SINGING--
An Extension of Speech

by

RUSSELL A. HAMMAR

The Scarecrow Press, Inc.
Metuchen, N.J. & London
1978

Library of Congress Cataloging in Publication Data

Hammar, Russell A
  Singing, an extension of speech.

  Includes index.
  1. Singing--Instruction and study. I. Title.
MT820.H23   784.9'32   78-11756
ISBN 0-8108-1182-0

This book
is affectionately dedicated
to my wife,
and to all of my students
who have encouraged me
to assemble my thoughts in writing

ACKNOWLEDGMENTS

I wish to express my sincere appreciation to Harvey Ringel, editor, NATS Bulletin, and Meribeth Bunch, Ph. D., voice consultant, for their critical comments concerning this book. (However, my statements do not necessarily reflect their views.) Thanks also to Bruce Apel, internationally known baritone, for his helpful and encouraging comments on an early draft of the manuscript. Special thanks are expressed to James J. Van Hare, M. D., and Nancy VanderLinde for their excellent illustrations.

I wish also to thank Eleanor VanderLinde for her many hours of typing, editing and proofreading of the manuscript.

I want especially to take this opportunity to thank my wife for her patience and support, as well as for the long hours of proofreading and suggestions.

Finally, I want to express my appreciation to the Kalamazoo College administration and faculty for their support, as well as for the released time and funding, which assisted me in completing this book.

R. H.
August 1978

TABLE OF CONTENTS

TABLE OF ILLUSTRATIONS

vi

INTRODUCTION

Any voice teacher who attempts to verbalize in print about his or her "method" or approach to vocal study risks a certain amount of misunderstanding. There are many possible ways of describing a particular phenomenon or sensation that is experienced in the act of singing. Also, it is one matter to teach voice in a studio situation, or to use effective vocal pedagogical techniques in a choral rehearsal, and quite another to explain in print outside the "laboratory" how it is done. No doubt, this phenomenon is influenced by the fact that each person brings to any situation his own set of word-pictures and interpretations, and thus it is impractical to expect that one individual's explanation of a particular phenomenon--especially the act of singing--is equally understandable to all readers. Moreover, singing is first an art and secondly a science. As a science it is in its infancy, and vocal scientists are constantly making new discoveries which should assist us in understanding the vocal mechanism and its functioning. (See Victor Alexander Fields, Foundations of a Singer's Art [New York: Vantage Press, 1977], p. 3.) Many assumptions of the past are now held in disrepute, while other older concepts of vocal pedagogy are still being used effectively. I do not profess to be a "vocal scientist." On the other hand, some basic concepts concerning the vowel in vocal production, stemming from more than thirty years' work in the vocal field, have motivated me to

1

expound my approach to the singing process. Many of my voice students have given me impetus for writing this book by such comments as, "Your approach is just good, common sense! Why don't you put it in writing?" More specifically, a student of mine in the seminary where I taught, said, "Your gospel of the vowel should be heard abroad!" So, in spite of the problem of semantics, I have attempted to define and explain what I believe to be the fundamental causes of good and poor vocal production as I understand them. Secondly, I have offered my solutions, which I hope will aid all students of voice and their teachers to develop insights into the basic problems in singing.

My theories and practice have evolved over a period of a career which has included experience on the concert stage, radio, television and recordings, as well as working with private vocal students, church and school choirs of all ages, and community choruses. My method has been applied to students of voice on all levels of experience, training and "natural ability," under conditions usually demanding results in a short period of time. Further inspiration to write about the "gospel of the vowel" has come from reading similar as well as opposing views about voice production.

My system of vocal pedagogy eliminates many of the traditional, extraneous vocalises (vocal calisthenics) which develop vocal prowess, but usually have little or no correlation with the actual problems found in the music on which the student is working. (Advanced voice development warrants the use of extensive vocalises when the singer has progressed far enough to use them correctly.) This notion is illustrated and reinforced by the use of an analogy. A golfer can strengthen and develop his muscles considerably--

even to the degree of becoming musclebound--by systematic calisthenics and weight lifting. Analogously, a singer can develop great strength and facility in his vocal musculature through rigorous study of vocalises. However, all of this muscle-building and training of itself will be of little use to the golfer in actually playing the game if there is no correct visual image in his mind, or to the vocalist in singing a song if there is no correct aural image in the ear of the singer. While the aspiring athlete and singer need to grow stronger physically, they really need specific instruction as to how to coordinate their muscles to function with maximum efficiency. Any exercises incorporated in reaching this goal should be directly correlated with the various aspects of muscle coordination. Brute force hardly makes a good golfer. Likewise, the singer who can vocalize loud, long and high, may actually have poor vocal production in singing a song. Therefore, the singer needs instruction that is directly correlated with the song being sung.

Frequently, advanced students beginning study with me have claimed that they could vocalize rapidly over a span of several octaves usually on the vowel "AH" or "AY." More often than not, these "vocal gymnasts," vocalizing to a high "c" or above, could not sustain their high pitches with any degree of good vocal tone. Their rapid vocalization did not permit them to realize how poor their singing production was. This type of spastic exercise can lead to very bad vocal habits, since the singer is "stabbing" at tones rather than "placing" them properly through an intelligent and careful approach.

As a matter of fact, some "armchair thinking" about the aural image (the sounds) which the singer wishes to produce would be far more beneficial than hours of thoughtless practicing. "Empty-headed" practice merely reinforces bad habits, rather than solving them. Ideally, a singer should have some insight into solving his problems before attempting to practice, for the act of singing is a very complex combination of body and mind. We cannot see the vocal instrument itself, and, consequently, we must rely upon analogies and word pictures for illustration. It is the aural image, rather than the visual image that orders the production of vocal tones. Much is left, then, to our imagination in voice production, and a thoughtful approach to the act of singing should be the goal of every singer. The mind must control the voice. One could say that good singing is an intellectual exercise. Victor Fields, in his excellent book Foundations of the Singer's Art discusses "principle versus practice." He states that principles denote "beginning" (a foundation). They are the laws governing practices: "When principles are violated, practices and actions become aimless and fruitless" (pp. 6-7).

According to the late James L. Mursell, music educator and psychologist, development of skill is the result (not the cause) of the many "avenues" of musical growth. (See his Education for Musical Growth [Boston: Ginn, 1948], chapters V-VIII.) These avenues can be described as:

1 Awareness (identifying a particular problem or phenomenon)

2 Initiative (responding to the problem or phenomenon)

3 Discrimination (determining what may be preferable over what one has been doing ... or recognizing the more efficient over the less efficient)

4 Insight (realizing the correct action to take--"aha, I see the light!")

INTRODUCTION

5 <u>Skill</u> (the result of the above progression!)

Skill in a given area cannot be developed in isolation and then superimposed upon the problem(s) at hand with optimum results. <u>The</u> <u>skill</u> <u>must</u> <u>be</u> <u>learned</u> <u>in</u> <u>the</u> <u>context</u> <u>of</u> <u>the</u> <u>situation</u> <u>in</u> <u>which</u> <u>it</u> <u>is</u> <u>to</u> <u>be</u> <u>used</u> if it is to have most meaningful results. This idea is substantiated by the meticulous efforts of space scientists to simulate the actual conditions of space as they train on earth.

If the literature being studied is chosen at the particular singer's level of development (yet is difficult enough to challenge him to grow), the actual music can be the primary pedagogical means to vocal development, whether it be in the vocal studio or the choral rehearsal. (Many choral directors spend from five to fifteen minutes of every rehearsal "developing" the voices through boring and meaningless vocalises.) The point need not be labored that the singing instructor must have a comprehensive knowledge of the best vocal literature for all levels of vocal development. How much more beneficial would it be for all concerned if the vocalises were garnered from the existing problems, and the music itself utilized to improve the vocal habits of the singer or singers.

This book, then, is not a manual of rote learning. Rather, it is a <u>pragmatic</u> <u>approach</u> <u>to</u> <u>gaining</u> <u>insights</u> <u>into</u> <u>the</u> <u>phenomenon</u> <u>of</u> <u>singing</u>. It is especially prepared for the vocal student who desires an uncomplicated description of the process of singing. My phonetic system of singing also has been introduced to and used successfully with many singers of advanced standing, particularly in problem areas such as the <u>passaggio</u>, breath management, and tonal consistency. It is my wish that this approach to vocalization will effectively

5

aid both teachers and students of voice. Moreover, this
treatise is an attempt to illustrate graphically that singing
is, in one sense, an extension of speech. That is to say,
proper formation of the buccalpharyngeal cavity (all the
areas in the mouth which shape a particular vowel) is the
basic action which the singer must utilize.

The basic theme of this entire treatise is to emphasize that good tone in speech or in singing is made through
pure vowel production, and that an accurate aural image of
the tones to be produced is essential to good singing. In my
teaching efforts, I use the vowel concept as the basis of
singing rather than referring to vowels as merely a part of
the diction phase of singing. We all recognize that singing
is more complicated than speaking, in that singing requires
more oral space than speaking. Also, one must sustain
sounds for arbitrary lengths of time in singing, whereas in
speaking, one merely retains the vowel sound long enough to
establish its meaning within the context of the word or sentence. Finally, singing requires a much wider range of tone
production, and, consequently, there are many more problems
in achieving the correct formation of each vowel sound for
the respective pitches. It seems logical to conclude, then,
that both effective speaking and good singing emanate from
the concept of pure vowel production.

Certainly, I recognize that I do not know all there is
to know about the voice and its production of sound. All
singers and teachers should be cognizant of the fact that
they learn daily from their experiences and application of
their intellect. Yet, there are certain facets in one's life
experience which are arresting, and, therefore, these factors
prompt one to examine one's own perceptions in a very spe-

cial manner. The writing of this book was generated by my years of teaching and singing--the "arresting experiences" which prompted me to try to pass on to others what I have found to be successful in the studio and in the choral rehearsal.

Some readers may consider me to be a maverick. I admit that I am and probably always will be one. Most of my conclusions about vocal production have developed from my own pursuit of unanswered questions (from voice teachers), through reading, research and empirical experimentation.

Many points will purposely be repeated to reinforce my basic concepts. These items underscore the emphases which, ideally, should become natural, subconscious thought processes in singing.

My remarks are dedicated to the vocal students of all levels who wish to have an uncomplicated description of the physical functioning of the voice and the process of singing. Many details of the anatomy and processes of singing are purposely omitted in an attempt to avoid confusion. However, there is no reason why singers should not study the vocal anatomy more thoroughly as they continue to develop.

Do not look, necessarily, for traditional guidelines for singing in this treatise. Instead, attempt to ferret out for yourself the elements of truth as they appear to you and then try them in your own laboratory--the practice room, the studio or the choral rehearsal--always adapting them to your own style and needs.

Chapter I

THE IMPORTANCE OF THE VOWEL
IN VOCAL PRODUCTION

Almost every article or book striving to deal with
vocal production recognizes that the vowel is important--
even vital--to proper tone production. Many vocal pedagogs
pay lip-service to the value or usefulness of the vowel in
singing, and then proceed to ignore application of the vowel
in their instructional efforts. Reference to the "open throat"
and "deeply-set-vowels" is quite common. What do these
terms mean? It seems that what is needed is a clearer understanding of the function of the vowel in vocal production;
the central objective proving that "good voweling" is the basis
of all good tone production.

The logical place to begin an analysis of the singing
process is through determining the character of the sound
that is to be made. What is our first clue? It is the premise that the correct formation of the vowel in the buccalpharyngeal cavity (the main amplifier) is the first step toward improving the sound. The correct vowel formation provides the proper size and shape of the buccalpharyngeal cavity (throat and mouth) during the act of speaking or singing.
There must be proper coordination between the sound begun
by the phonation (action) of the vocal folds and its amplifi-
cation--the resonators. Cornelius Reid supports this concept:

9

Vowels are of particular interest throughout training. Tonal impurities are easily detectable there,
as well as misconcepts [sic] in the area of pronunciation and quality.... A vowel will only be as
pure as the coordinative process will allow. Consequently, work on the vowel must move toward
two major functional objectives: 1) it must improve the resonance adjustment, i.e., eliminate
constrictor tensions, and 2) it must assist in making changes in the registration.... The best way
to study the behavior patterns of vowels is to con-
struct an exercise wherein all primary vowels are
included so that they represent the changing factor
in an otherwise stable environment.[1]

Reid pursues this idea further with:

This can be done quite easily by using a single
tone and maintaining a constant level of intensity,
while linking the five primary vowels together as
'ah,' 'ay,' 'ee,' 'oh,' and 'oo.'[2]

This concept directly supports my use of the Vowel
Spectrum as a basic vocalise and the core of my vocal pedagogy in Chapter III. (See especially page 69.)

The notion that singing is sustained speech is also a
widely accepted premise. (Unfortunately, the concept of
singing as an extension of good speech habits is more frequently ignored in practice than it is applied.) Historically,
vocal authorities have recognized that the Italian language is
the purest in sound and the least complicated of all languages
to sing.

Without doubt, the Italian language, with its wealth
of vowels is better adapted for singing than the
German language, so rich in consonants, or any
other language. The organs of speech and the
vocal apparatus, in the Italian language, are less
subjected to violent form-modifications.[3]

The ability to discern the pure vowel form is sad-
ly neglected by singers other than the Latin race

10

[sic]. The Italian, for instance, has keenest ear
for perfect tones.... This is a result of their
language. [4]

One should approach the singing of all languages, by
employing clear, simple vowel sounds with a "softening" of
plosive consonants. In other words, vowels in singing should
be pure and precise; the consonants should be elegant and
free from constriction.

Furthermore, the notion that singing is an extension
of speech has been supported historically by vocal authorities.

Voice is speech, and is produced by the mouth,
not by the vocal cords. The vocal cords produce
only sounds, which are transformed into vowels
and consonants by a phonetic process taking place
in the mouth, and giving origin to the voice. [5]

By the term "mouth," it is assumed that Dr. Marafioti here means the entire buccalpharyngeal cavity.

Gertrude Beckman, in her book, Tools for Speaking
and Singing, says "Sing as you speak ... IF you speak
well."[6] Marafioti again calls attention to the notion that
speech and singing are related:

Even the highest pitches of the singing voice will
present no difficulties when their production is per-
formed along the track of the speaking voice. [7]

... most of the failures in the singing profession
are due to the ignorance of the important role
played by the speaking voice in relation to the art
of singing. [8]

... singing must first be saying. [9]

What has happened in recent years of scientific understanding of the functioning of the vocal instrument is a be-
nign neglect of the application of the vowel in singing. I
would like the reader to examine with me what I believe to

be a return to the image of the pure vowel as the basis of all
refined singing, for in the pursuit of scientific truths about
the functioning of the vocal mechanism, there has been a
tendency to disregard the role of the pure vowel in voice
production. During the period of the "Golden Age of Song"
of the 16th and 17th centuries (sometimes referred to as the
bel canto era), the emphasis was placed upon the purity of
the vowel and careful treatment of consonants. Moreover,
every voice teacher should insist that his students continue
to be conscious of good speech habits, because clearly articulated speech readily leads to clearly articulated singing.
In short, singing and speech emanate from the same source.

Perhaps there will be those readers who will ask,
Does this pure vowel concept rule out vowel modification?
I believe that vowel modification is a result of certain adjustments or formations of the oral pharynx and tongue, not the
cause. That is, when the singer imagines the pure qualities
of each vowel on any given pitch, the correct adjustments
should take place more readily, even though the vowel on the
upper note becomes modified in comparison with the lower
note. If one experiments by singing any vowel while employing an octave glissando, he will note that in order to produce
an acceptable sound on the upper note he must make an adjustment of the tongue and oral pharynx by adding more space.
At this point one must not confuse cause and effect. It is
true that as space is added to the buccalpharyngeal cavity on
higher notes, the vowel becomes modified. For instance,
the vowel "EE" on g^2 begins to resemble "ih." However,
the singer should always think the "EE" vowel clearly, merely adding the necessary space to accommodate the vocal process efficiently. In my teaching and singing experience, when

12

the singer's aural image envisions the "ih" instead of the "EE," the tone tends to become too heavy and unfocused. The important ingredient in the thought process should be for the singer to maintain the aural image of the core of the vowel sound with which he started--assuming it was a good sound in the beginning of the experiment. If the mind is confused, the tone will be diffused.

> Basically it is the mind that sings, not the voice. You can say or sing only what you think. Therefore, you sing only as beautiful a tone as you can think, since your voice always follows your thought [aural image]. [10]

However, it is of utmost importance at this juncture to cite the fact that we cannot hear our own voices as they really sound. We know what a shock it is to hear our voices, particularly in speech, played back to us on a tape recorder. In other words, there is an auditory and sensory conflict between the singer and the listener. [11] This is caused by the fact that we tend to hear our own voices through the auditory (Eustachian) tubes, which connect the nasopharynx with each inner ear.

This concept seems to support the conclusion that a clearly envisioned aural image of the vowel(s) to be produced can be most helpful to the singer in his attempt to shape the buccalpharyngeal cavity correctly in order to produce proper amplification of the sounds initiated by the vibrator. Naturally, this assumes that there is an absence of undue tension in the vocal musculature.

In instructing individuals or groups in singing, I have found that when singers are given a clue as to how to shape the buccalpharyngeal cavity through the spoken vowel, the

13

tone quality, diction, blend (ensemble balance), flexibility, intonation and volume improve noticeably. If one clearly understands this theory, the shape of the vowel can be formed more correctly and instinctively. There are many varieties of mouth shapes and sizes, but man is endowed with the flexibility in the mouth and throat cavities to produce relatively common sounds (unless nature has erred in some cases, such as creating individuals with malformed palates). Granted, some persons are endowed with stronger and more flexible throat and vocal muscles than others. These more "talented" singers are those who usually become outstanding vocalists, because they can adjust the oral pharynx to a wider variety of nuances of vowel sizes and shapes than the average person and they also possess better coordination in the vocal musculature.

Quality or kind of vowel, then, is largely determined by the shape of the buccalpharyngeal cavity in relation to the sound produced by the vocal folds. The shape of the resonator is changed by varying the positions of the tongue, jaw, soft palate, lips and larynx. The lips have an effect upon resonance directly in proportion to their tension. That is, tense lip formations transfer muscularly down into the larynx and thus impede action of the vocal muscles. Even the slightest movements of these muscles modify the form of this cavity, and thus a great variety of sounds and sound-colors is possible.

Barrows and Pierce support the theory of correct vowel formation:

> Since the vowel is the primary vocal element in speech and song, the voice depends largely upon it for beauty, carrying power and expressiveness. [12]

14

THE VOWEL

Normally, the mind will direct the correct throat formation for a given vowel on a given pitch if the mind clearly understands what vowel sound is required. For instance, when singers confuse the "ih" sound (as in the word "gift") with the "eh" sound (as in "get"), their quality of sound usually suffers, and diction becomes less clear. Whenever there is indecision as to what vowel sound needs to be produced, the voice loses its focal point and intensity. The correct cavity (in size and shape), devoid of muscular tension, permits the natural functioning of the vocal folds, thus permitting a natural vibrato to be present in the voice.

Further establishing the notion that vowel shape and size are primary factors in vocal production, the following opinions of Weldon Whitlock substantiate the importance of the pure vowel production in singing:

> We see, quite definitely, that the great bel canto teachers required four specific things from their pupils: first, absolutely pure vowels; second, the ability to sing a long, smooth phrase, unbroken; third, the execution of simple ornamentation and then elaborate fioratura, and fourth, the complete mastery of recitative. [13]

> It must be remembered that today we seldom hear an absolutely pure vowel, and when we hear it and produce it, it will sound quite radical. One cannot be too radical in the purity of any vowel. [14]

> The singer should 'perceive' the pure vowel, then go instantly to the heart of the vowel, and stay there as long as notation permits, then going instantly to the heart of the next pure vowel.... The vowel is the conductor of sound, while the consonant is a non-conductor. The vowel has pitch, while the consonant does not.... [15]

In other words, the sound will be good if the resonating cavities of the mouth and throat are the correct shape and size to amplify the overtones produced by the fundamental tone--assuming that tension does not exist in the vocal muscles.

The late Charles Kennedy Scott, prominent British vocal authority, also gave considerable support to this theory:

> It is common experience that pupils do not recognize or appreciate the vowel quality that the professor may pattern, till they can produce it themselves. Then, all is clear.[16]
>
> If the cavity is right, the sound will be right.... The perfect cavity makes the perfect vowel.[17]

The shape of the "horn" (buccalpharyngeal cavity) then, governs the amplification of the sound waves made from the vibrating folds. The singer must "speak" (form) the vowel in its proper size and shape subconsciously before he begins to produce the tone which is to be sung.

How, then, does the student achieve a clearer understanding of the vowel? First, we must establish the concept that the clear, correctly-produced vocal tone must have only one vowel sound as a focal point on any given note or series of notes. For instance, singers are often heard to combine diphthongs or darken all vowels into nondescript sounds which are difficult to distinguish from one another. The result of this phenomenon is poor diction and inefficient vocal production. One hears singers form the English vowel "I" as "uh," "ih" as "EE" ("keeng" for "king") and "OH" as "aw" ("gaw" for "go"). Tongue, throat and jaw tension cause malformation of vowels, resulting in "pinched" tones. Oversized vowels as well should be considered malformed. It is possible also for extreme tongue tension to prevent the singer from achieving proper vowel production; i.e., the tongue bunched up in the back of the throat when attempting

16

to sing high notes. This tension transfers down into the laryngeal area and impedes free action of the vocal muscles. As cited above, mixing the "AH" and "EE" sounds of the English vowel "I" (diphthong), illustrates clearly the example of a malformed vowel. This malformation of the "I" vowel usually results in producing the sound of "uh"--or even "oy" in some extreme cases. Note how the tongue becomes tense when "AH" and "EE" are mixed. Now, pronounce a clear "AH" as in the Italian language, the vanishing "EE" vowel coming at the conclusion of the sound emission. Note that the tongue tends to lie flatter in the floor of the mouth on the "AH" vowel. The correct approach is to retain the first of the two vowel sounds of any diphthong for almost the entire duration of the note. The second sound of the diphthong is then used to conclude the word or to join with the consonant (if there is one) in finishing the word. This matter will be discussed more fully in Chapter III, when the Vowel Spectrum is introduced.

Scott again admonishes the singer, "Beware of sticking in diphthongs all over the place--a sure sign of poor singing....[18]

The Italian language generally does not encounter the problem of diphthongs. That language has mostly strong and weak vowel sounds, and these vowels are rarely mixed as are diphthongs found in the English language. (Italian diphthongs are always spelled phonetically. In other words, all printed sounds should be articulated.) The Italian may emphasize one vowel sound over another (strong or weak), but these sounds are almost always distinctive and identifiable. For instance, the word "guardo" (to look) is pronounced "goo - AH - rolled 'r' - doh." The "OO" and the "AH" are never mixed or run together and there is no vanishing "OO" sound (diphthong) in the Italian language.

Distorted vocal production occurs when the singer does not understand that the vowel sounds have varying sizes and shapes on varying pitches. A malformed vowel may be too large or too small if the size of the oral pharynx is too small and/or too wide; or the size may be too large to accommodate a focused tone on a given pitch. For instance, singers too often produce a "woofy" (dark) tone on medium and low pitches of their vocal range. This is invariably the result of a throat size and shape which is larger than necessary for the particular height of that pitch. This latter example typifies over-sized, out of focus vowel formation.

While the singer must keep in mind that slightly more room must be made in the buccalpharyngeal cavity for each given vowel sound as the scale is ascended, the shape of each vowel must also remain narrow and "forward" to avoid spreading the tone. Moreover, one's mind should always focus sharply upon the essential core of the sound to be produced. One useful analogy is to imagine a narrow channel in which all vowels must be confined and not to permit the vowel focus to spread outside of this channel regardless of the height of the pitch. Concurrently, the singer should pinpoint the image of the vowel continuously as he ascends the scale. This tends to avoid the wide-open, spread tone, which so many singers are apt to produce as they ascend the scale into the upper regions of the voice.

> ... [T]he singer, by his art, can ... give a very fair representation of any vowel throughout the compass of his voice.... The problem is to keep the same, or much the same, resonance, as the voice

rises or falls; i.e., to keep the same vowel as
far as possible. [19]

By keeping the "same vowel," we must recognize that
it is the same vowel to the listener. This, of course, means
that there is constant change in the size and shape of the buccalpharyngeal cavity as the singer ascends and descends
through the scope of his vocal range. For example, the
"EE" vowel over an octave span requires noticeably more
space on the upper note than on the lower note. However,
the change is almost imperceptible when ascending or descending by half or even whole steps.

The singer can achieve the objective "dans la masque"
("forward" focus of the tone in the facial mask) by releasing
the jaw of all tension while projecting the sound as one would
do in public speaking (oratory). The admonition should be:
speak it; then sing it immediately along the speech track
with the same forward projection, being certain that the
vowel has reasonable depth as well as definite focus. An
effective illustration for the student is to imagine that the
sound is projected (aimed) at a distant point with the jaw
completely released of tension; a feeling of "out and down."
The jaw should "hang loose" as though it were attached by
rubber bands which allow it to "seek its own level," rather
than being jammed down to make space. The soft palate
should make the necessary space.

The most important point to be emphasized in this
approach to vocal pedagogy is that efficient vocal production
requires the singer to be cognizant of the fact that pure
vowel sounds (backed by proper space in the oral pharynx)
are the route to pure, balanced tones.

Many of the shallow tones produced by chorus singers

are basically <u>right</u>, but are incomplete! That is to say,
what the singer needs to do in this case is to add a "slight
yawn" to that shallow formation: a lifting of the soft palate
<u>without</u> <u>distorting</u> <u>the</u> <u>vowel</u> <u>from</u> <u>its</u> <u>central</u> <u>focus</u> (forma-
tion).

Efficient voweling accomplishes several ideal objectives in vocal production in addition to producing better tone
quality:

> Improves intonation, because the vowel formants con-
> tain a combination of higher and lower partials.
>
> Increases volume, resulting from proper formants of
> each characteristic vowel.
>
> Improves diction by providing the projection of the text
> in a meaningful manner.
>
> Develops flexibility of tone for fast passages.
>
> Permits the voice to blend with other singers in en-
> semble singing.
>
> Aids in balancing sections in ensemble work.
>
> Extends the range of the singer.

The English language is generally regarded as not
being phonetic because of its confusing vowel sounds--words
spelled differently, but pronounced the same: "here and
hear," "know and no," "need and knead," "bough" of a tree
and "bow" to an audience, etc. Also, some words are
spelled the same and pronounced differently: "house" (to
live in) and to "house" someone, "collect" (accumulate) and
"collect" (brief formal prayer), to "read" and to have
"read," "the" before a consonant and "the" (EE) before a
vowel, etc.

Still more confusing to the singer of the English language (particularly if English is not his native tongue) are
homonyms--words whose pronunciation is different from that

the vowel indicates by its spelling, for example:

The Italian vowel "a" -- AH (ah, "ah")†

father - AH (longest duration) ⎫
mother - ah (shorter duration) ⎬ Three forms of
the - "ah" (shortest duration) ⎭ the "AH" vowel
heart - AH
night - AH + vanishing ee
thy - AH + vanishing ee
how - AH + vanishing oo
row - (argument) AH + vanishing oo
opposite - ah and "ah" (see Vowel Spectrum p. 69)

The Italian vowel "u" -- OO†

truly -- OO
put - uuh (short form of "OO" vowel)
but - "ah" (shortest form of AH)

The Italian "o" vowel -- OH†

over - OH
ode - OH
dog - aw
loathe - OH
row - OH (row a boat)

†Some of these pronunciations may appear to be contrary at times to the standard International Phonetic Alphabet (IPA). I do not use the IPA, because, in applying the minute particulars of that precise phonetic alphabet, the singer tends to become restricted by detail, thus losing the sense of freedom necessary for good vocal production. Furthermore, for the student unacquainted with the IPA system, learning it is an added chore en route to improved singing. The results achieved by the Vowel Spectrum (see page 69) are essentially the same as those of the IPA when applied to the singing process. This simplified vowel identification stems from the language itself and does not require learning another alphabetical set.

One must be careful to envisage the correct vowel sound of the many homonyms found in the English language. Therefore, careful identification of these sounds as they pertain to pure vowel sounds is of vital importance to the singer.

21

The above examples reveal the great need for the singer to have a clear concept (aural image) of the <u>vowel sound</u> that must be produced in singing. The application of the Vowel Spectrum will be developed in detail in Chapter III.

References

[1] Cornelius L. Reid, <u>Voice: Psyche and Soma</u> (New York: Joseph Patelson Music House, 1975), pp. 64-65.

[2] Ibid., p. 65.

[3] Lilli Lehman, <u>How to Sing</u> (New York: Macmillan, 1952), p. 215.

[4] Franz Proschowsky, <u>The Way to Sing</u> (Boston: C. C. Birchard, 1923), p. 65.

[5] P. Mario Marafioti, M.D., <u>Caruso's Method of Voice Production</u> (New York: W. Appelton, 1923; reprint, Austin: Cadica Enterprises, 1958), p. 50.

[6] Gertrude Beckman, <u>Tools for Speaking and Singing</u> (New York: G. Schirmer, 1929), p. 84.

[7] Marafioti, <u>Caruso's Method</u>, p. 134.

[8] Ibid., ·p. 165.

[9] Ibid., p. 185.

[10] Victor Alexander Fields, <u>Foundations of the Singer's Art</u> (New York: Vantage Press, 1977), p. 13.

[11] Dwayne Jorgenson, "The Mirror Image in Singing," <u>NATS Bulletin</u>, October 1976, p. 46.

[12] Sarah T. Barrows and Anne E. Pierce, <u>The Voice: How to Use It</u> (Boston: Expression Co., 1932), p. 85.

[13] Weldon Whitlock, <u>Facets of the Singer's Art</u>, vol. 1 of Twentieth Century Masterworks on Singing, Edward

Foreman, General Editor (Champaign, Ill.: Pro Musica Press, 1967), p. 23.

[14]Ibid., p. 24.

[15]Ibid., p. 25.

[16]Charles Kennedy Scott, The Fundamentals of Singing (London: Cassell, 1954), p. 217.

[17]Ibid., p. 218.

[18]Ibid., p. 139.

[19]Ibid., p. 257.

CHAPTER II

THE VOCAL ANATOMY

The vocal mechanism is such a small and exceptionally complex organ of the body, and its interwoven musculature is so intricate, that the "complete instrument" is extremely difficult to illustrate in photographs, drawings or X-rays. Therefore, some of the specific musculature and cartilaginous areas must be deleted in illustrations in order to present the basic contour and action of the laryngeal mechanism.

An exhaustive analysis of this intricate set of bones, muscles, cartilages and ligaments may be found in many of the books to which I refer in this chapter. (Recommended books that describe the vocal mechanism in greater detail are such as Gray's Anatomy, Appelman's The Science of Vocal Pedagogy, Luchsinger and Godfrey's Voice-Speech-Language, Vennard's Singing; The Mechanism and Technic and Rose's The Singer and the Voice.)

My objective here is to describe the "instrument" only in its basic manner of functioning, so that the essential components of the "singing mechanism" can be better understood.

An understanding of the physiology of the voice cannot be applied directly to the singing process. However, a more accurate imagery can be helpful by indirection. Specifically, it can provide insights into and respect for the overall vocal production process. If the vocalist possesses an understand-

(continued on page 28)

24

Figure 1

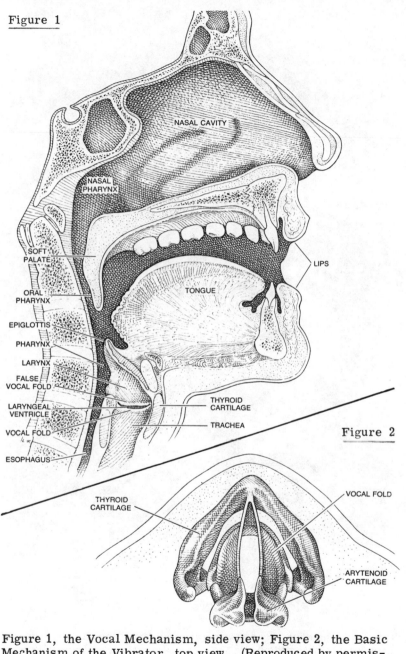

Figure 1, the Vocal Mechanism, side view; Figure 2, the Basic Mechanism of the Vibrator, top view. (Reproduced by permission from Johan Sundberg's "The Acoustics of the Singing Voice," Scientific American, March 1977. Copyright © 1977 by Scientific American, Inc.)

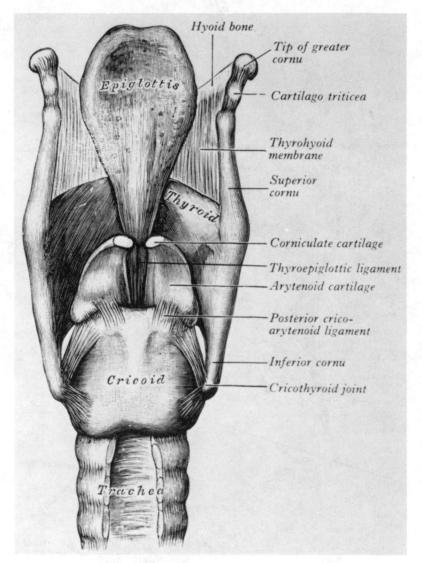

Figure 3A

The Ligaments of the Larynx, viewed from the rear. (Reproduced by permission from Gray's Anatomy, 35th British edition.)

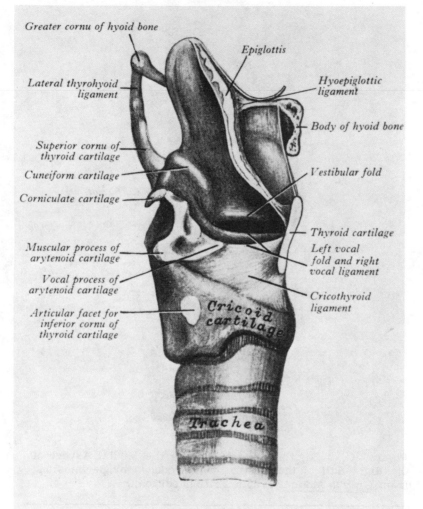

Greater cornu of hyoid bone

Epiglottis

Lateral thyrohyoid ligament

Hyoepiglottic ligament

Body of hyoid bone

Superior cornu of thyroid cartilage

Cuneiform cartilage

Vestibular fold

Corniculate cartilage

Muscular process of arytenoid cartilage

Thyroid cartilage

Left vocal fold and right vocal ligament

Vocal process of arytenoid cartilage

Articular facet for inferior cornu of thyroid cartilage

Cricothyroid ligament

Cricoïd cartilage

Trachea

Figure 3B

A Dissection to Show the Right Half of the Cricothyroid Ligament; right lamina of the thyroid cartilage and the subjacent muscles have been removed. (Reproduced by permission from Gray's Anatomy, 35th British edition.)

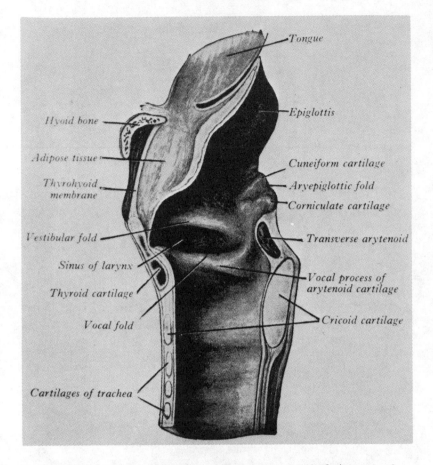

Figure 3C, a Sagittal Section Showing the Medial Aspect of the Right Half of the Larynx. (Reproduced by permission from Gray's Anatomy, 35th British edition.)

ing (including a mental picture) of how his vocal mechanism operates, he should be able to better understand the problems of and solutions to improving his singing efforts. Ideally, a more realistic image of the functioning of the vocal "instrument" should be followed by explicit instructions as to how to allow the complete vocal organ to perform.

VOCAL ANATOMY

One may assign the areas of the vocal mechanism to
three primary categories: (1) the vibrator (oscillator), (2)
the resonators (amplifier) and (3) the respiratory apparatus
(power supply) along with the muscles directly involved in
breathing.

THE VIBRATOR AND ITS MUSCLES

The vocal folds (vocal lips and vocal bands), which
initiate vocal sounds, lie horizontally across the larynx
(voice box) from front to back. The larynx is sometimes
dubbed the "Adam's Apple" in men and "Eve's Orange" (or
"Eve's Peach") in women. The vocal bands (ligaments)
and thyroarytenoid muscles are attached together to form
the vibrating unit and their action is much like a valve.
Together they form the vocal folds. They are fastened to
the anterior (front) of the larynx and open (abduct) for breath
inhalation and close (adduct) for swallowing, speaking, singing and lifting heavy objects. (However, in speaking and
singing the vocal folds open and close to produce sounds,
whereas in swallowing and in lifting heavy objects the folds
remain tightly closed.) The fibers of the vocalis muscle
crisscross each other in a confusing manner, and thus,
simple descriptions of their functioning action are difficult
to understand or explain.

The vocal folds are the laryngeal muscles primarily responsible for vocal production. They are two inter-twined
sets of muscles, called the thyroarytenoid and the vocalis
muscles (see Fig. 4). These muscles may be termed the
"tensors," and they are regarded as being the inner body
of the vocal fold.[1] The function of these tensors is to tighten

(The top of the diagram is the
back of the throat, the
bottom is the front.)

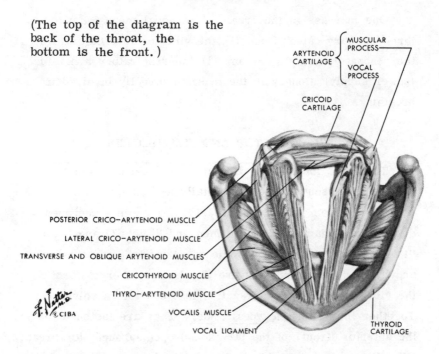

Figure 4, Intrinsic Muscles of the Larynx. (Reproduced by
permission from the Ciba Collection of Medical Illustrations
by Frank H. Netter, M.D. , © Ciba.)

the vocal folds--to hold the cords together (adduction) in
varying degrees in normal speaking and singing.

The posterior or back end of the thyroarytenoid muscles
are attached to two small (pyramid-shaped) arytenoid cartilages, which are mobile. They are pivoted by muscular
action of the three arytenoid muscles which control the
mechanism for breathing and the adjustment of the thickness
and length of the folds (cords) (stretching action)[2]:

> When the trans-arytenoid muscles are tensed, they
> draw the arytenoid cartilages together, thus helping
> to close the rear portion of the glottis (vocal folds).

When the lateral crico-arytenoid muscles are tensed, they draw the outer end of the arytenoid cartilage downwards and out to adduct (close) the vocal folds.

When the posterior (rear) crico-arytenoid muscles tense, they pull the arytenoid cartilages backwards and inwards in order to abduct (open) the vocal cords for breathing.[3]

It should be of interest to the serious student and teacher of voice to note that the average measurements of the larynx in adults are as follows:

Length in males: about 44 millimeters.

Length in females: about 36 millimeters.

Until puberty the larynx in the male differs little in size from the female. In the female its increase at puberty is only small. In the male the increase is considerable; all the cartilages enlarge and the thyroid cartilage projects in the anterior median line of the neck, while the anteroposterior diameter is nearly doubled.[4]

The vocal bands themselves are two pearly-white shelves of thin mucous membrane clothing the vocal ligaments, 15 millimeters long (about three-fifths of an inch) in adult males and 10 millimeters long (about two-fifths of an inch) in adult females.[5]

Thus, we should recognize what great expectations we make of this very small part of the human anatomy.

Caution: It is extremely important for any singer who is contemplating major surgery, to register concern with his surgeon (or anesthetist) about the insertion of a catheter through the larynx, the purpose of which is that respiration can continue unimpeded. There have been cases reported in which damage has been done to the vocal folds by careless insertion of the tube down the trachea. The small inflatable collar on the tube, which secures it properly, must be located below the vocal folds.

Despite our advanced contemporary means of observation of the vocal mechanism through photographing the larynx during the actual process of singing and speaking, there remains controversy over the action of the vocal folds in phonation.

Fields suggests that three interesting theories of glottal action have evolved from recent research in the field of vocal pedagogy and he suggests that all of them are valid to a certain degree and that we might consider them to be a combined phenomenon of triple action. [6] The three theories are:

First, the "neurochronaxic theory, which holds that frequency of vibration of the vocal cords [folds] at any given pitch is a direct result of a corresponding number of impulses transmitted along the recurrent nerve. This nerve supplies the numerous minute fibers of the vocalis muscle. Because these fibers terminate at the glottal ledge, the latter is caused to contract and relax rhythmically during phonation.... [W]e must 'hear' the pitch mentally to be able to sing it.... What we phonate is merely an imitation of what we hear" [aural image]. [7]

This theory cannot stand by itself. Rather, we might concede that it is preliminary, with the second and third items below being necessary components of this complex action of muscles, cartilages, ligaments and bones.

Second, the myoelastic theory claims that, when the vocal cords (folds) are closed, the subglottic air becomes compressed to such an extent that its mounting pressure explodes the glottal closure. At this moment the condensation of air is propagated through the oral cavity into the surrounding air. Following this explosive reduction of air pressure, the vocal folds are driven back into closed position through the elasticity of their contracted musculature. Subglottic pressure increases again and the process is repeated.

Third, the <u>aerodynamic</u> <u>theory</u> states that a) the thyroarytenoid muscles are adducted in a preparatory action; b) they are then adjusted to a given tension, mass and shape; while c) exhaled air causes a suction that draws the vocal lips more firmly together in what is called the Bernoulli effect. A continuous upward air pressure thus maintains the glottic closure through suction and also induces vibratory action by forcing an intermittent release of breath between the vocal edges. [9]

"(The Bernoulli effect is a lifting force in aviation; and it creates the suction needed in atomizers, as well as being a factor in the vibrators of wind instruments. ... If you will hold a letter-size sheet of paper against your chin and blow, the paper will rise to a horizontal position.... When the vocal folds are fairly close to each other, there is a narrowing of the air passage sufficient for the Bernoulli effect to draw them together, if the breath is flowing at the same time.)"[10]

The paper rises, because the air current blowing across the limp, hanging paper reduces the air pressure, permitting the pressure from below to push the paper up. If this action predominates in vocal production, there is less strain on the vocal folds.

The singer will be able to perceive some of the primary action of the vocal folds if he imagines the thyroarytenoid muscles to have a zipper-like action (see Fig. 5). While this analogy does not fully describe the functioning of the laryngeal muscles, it may help the singer to appreciate the

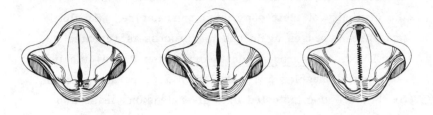

Figure 5, "Zipper" Action of the Vocal Bands, top view.
(Drawings by Nancy Vander Linde.)

---

basic action of the vocal mechanism. This zipper action is
especially evident in the falsetto or head voice range. Starting at the lowest part of the individual's range, the vocal
folds are relatively loose and thick. In the middle range,
the folds begin to stretch, and the entire length of the vocal
bands vibrate. Then, as the singer ascends the scale, the
"zipper" gradually closes. This is the damping or immobi-
lizing action, caused by the thyroarytenoid muscles as they
shorten the length of the vocal cords, until the action is ter-
minated at the highest pitch in his range. Simultaneously,
with proper singing technique, the vocal folds are also
stretched by action of the cricothyroid muscles as the singer
ascends the scale, so that, ideally, the vocal folds become
thinner and shorter as the pitch ascends. According to Reid,

> The adduction of the vocal folds is a process which
> finds the posterior portion of the cord meeting and
> pressing together, thus shortening the anterior seg-
> ment which has been left free to vibrate. An exact
> parallel to this process is the common zipper action
> which, when made to close, gradually reduces the
> aperture above the adducted parts. [11]

Luchsinger and Arnold also allude to this action by stating,

> With rising pitch, vocal cord amplitude and glottal closure diminish. As a result, the opening quotient of glottal closure diminishes with rising pitch. [12]

Rose states that as the pitch rises:

> ... [T]he tension on the vocal cords [folds] increases until a certain point when the tension becomes too great and further elevation in pitch is achieved in a manner similar to fingering a violin string on the finger-board, i. e., the posterior forward sections of the vocal cords are tightly adducted and the length of the vocal cord left free to vibrate is shortened.... As the higher tones are produced in a gradually ascending scale, the approximated posterior section becomes longer and longer and the vibrating portion correspondingly shorter. [13]

Finally, Brodnitz, in his book, <u>Keep Your Voice Healthy</u>, has photographs by Pressman which show three stages of the mechanism of the vocal folds:

> With increasing pitch the vocal cords become more approximated in the posterior part until, in the highest falsetto, only a small anterior segment is left free to vibrate. [14]

Some vocal pedagogs and scientists feel that the zipper description is inaccurate, because the action is not entirely analagous to the string (vocal band) shortening concept. However, if we analyze one of Appelman's statements, I believe the whole matter is put into perspective allowing us to

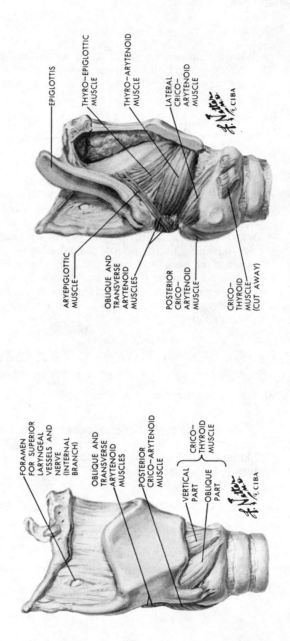

Left: Figure 6 and right: Figure 7, Intrinsic Muscles of the Larynx. From the Ciba Collection of Medical Illustrations by Frank H. Netter, M.D., © Ciba.

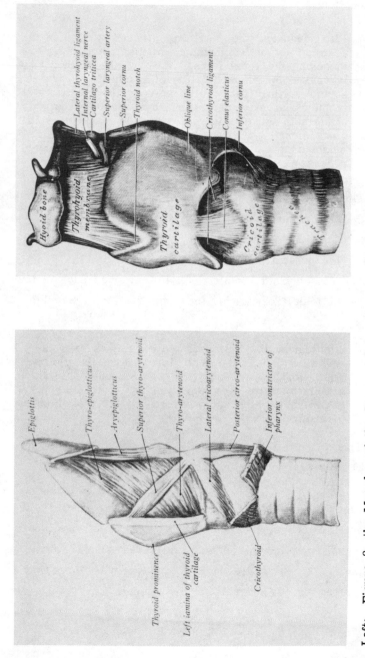

Left: Figure 8, the Muscles of the Larynx, left side view (most of the left thyroid cartilage has been removed). Right: Figure 9, the Ligaments of the Larynx, front-to-side view. Reproduced by permission from Gray's Anatomy, 35th British edition.

Figure 8 labels:
- Epiglottis
- Thyro-epiglotticus
- Aryepiglotticus
- Superior thyro-arytenoid
- Thyro-arytenoid
- Lateral cricoarytenoid
- Posterior circo-arytenoid
- Inferior constrictor of pharynx
- Thyroid prominence
- Left lamina of thyroid cartilage
- Cricothyroid

Figure 9 labels:
- Lateral thyrohyoid ligament
- Internal laryngeal nerve
- Cartilago triticea
- Superior laryngeal artery
- Superior cornu
- Thyroid notch
- Oblique line
- Cricohyoid ligament
- Conus elasticus
- Inferior cornu
- Hyoid bone
- Thyrohyoid membrane
- Thyroid cartilage
- Cricoid cartilage
- Trachea

interpret the zipper action in light of other factors bearing upon phonation:

> Pitch changes, then, are not directly attributed to a single act of lengthening, thinning, tightening or loosening the vocal folds. Rather, the pitch change is caused by the modulation of tracheal air pressure resulting from the changes in the elasticity of the vocal margins. It is thus assumed that the changes in the elasticity are caused by changes in mass, length, and tension of the thyro-arytenoid muscles in a synchronized act, a most complicated process ...[15] [emphasis added].

Therefore, we may summarize that in ascending a scale, thinning of the vocal mass takes place; that the vocal folds are dampened in the process; and that various degrees of tension are present.

The cricothyroid muscles pull the anterior ends of the glottis (vocal folds) forward by their contraction. (See Fig. 4.)

> Simultaneously, the arytenoid cartilages exert a backward pull at the posterior ends of the glottis. Thus, for any given pitch, each set of end muscles acts in opposite directions against a resisting internal contraction and stiffening of the glottal edges themselves.[16]

This pull stretches and thus thins out the mass of the vocal folds, permitting the singer to ascend to higher pitches.

Figures 6-9 are presented to acquaint the reader with the essential muscles, ligaments, cartilages and bones of the laryngeal area upon which the singer depends for vocal production. With these drawings we can begin to appreciate the complexity of this marvelous "instrument."

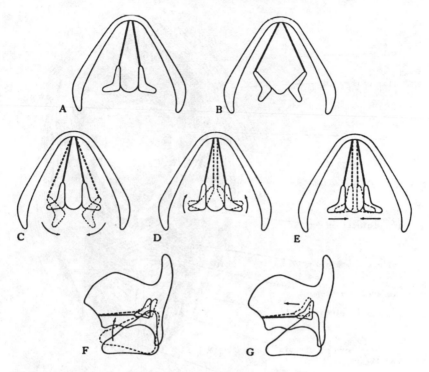

Figure 10, Action of the Vocal Folds as Manipulated by the Cricoarytenoid Cartilages. (Reproduced by permission from Gray's Anatomy, 35th British edition.)

The diagrams A through E of Fig. 10 illustrate how the vocal folds are manipulated by the muscles controlling the arytenoid cartilages for breathing and speaking or singing:

A. Position of the folds in quiet breathing.

B. Position of the folds in forced breathing: note how widely the folds are spread. This position is more extreme, but similar to the posture of the folds when inhaling with the so-called "open-throat" which singers are encouraged to maintain for large, full breath intake.

C. Abduction (drawing away) of the vocal folds for

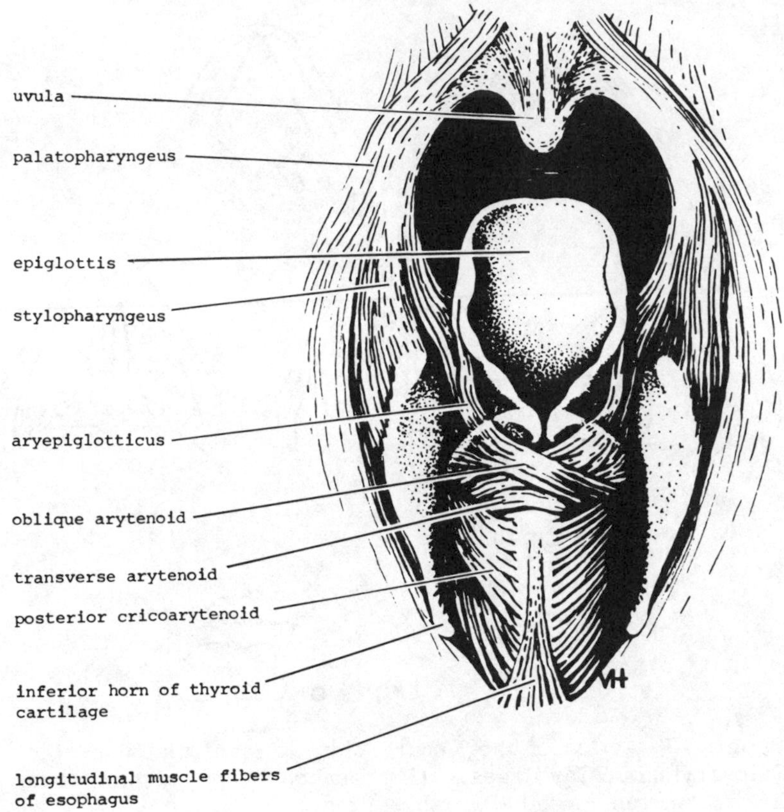

uvula

palatopharyngeus

epiglottis

stylopharyngeus

aryepiglotticus

oblique arytenoid

transverse arytenoid

posterior cricoarytenoid

inferior horn of thyroid cartilage

longitudinal muscle fibers of esophagus

Figure 11, the Larynx, seen from the rear. (Drawing by James J. Van Hare, M.D.)

quiet (normal) breathing and inhalation for singing: arrows indicate the lines of pull of the posterior (rear) cricoarytenoid muscles. Note the rotation of the two cricoarytenoid cartilages as shown by the dotted lines.

D. Adduction (drawing together) of the vocal folds for phonation by the arytenoid cartilages as they are governed by the lateral arytenoid and interarytenoid muscles.

E. Closure of the rima glottidis. The arrows indicate

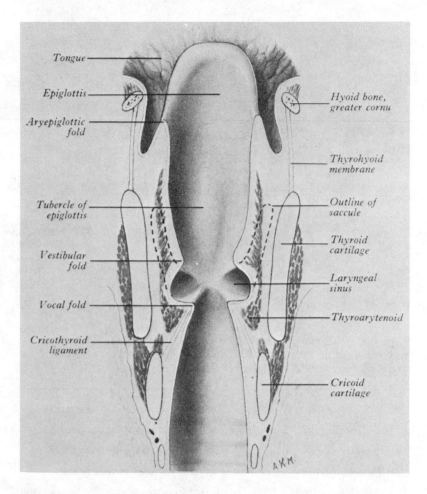

Figure 12, Cut-Away View of the Larynx, from the rear; a coronal section through the larynx and the cranial end of the Trachea. (Reproduced by permission from Gray's Anatomy, 35th British ed.)

the line of pull of the transverse arytenoid muscles. Both the vocal folds and the arytenoid cartilages are adducted, but there is no rotation of the latter [in this case for singing in the upper range of the voice].

41

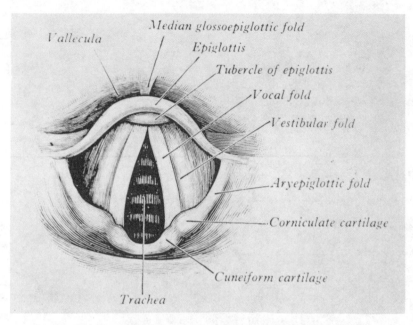

Figure 13, Laryngoscope View of the Vocal Mechanism, interior of the larynx. (Reproduced by permission from Gray's Anatomy, 35th British edition.)

F. Tension of the vocal folds, produced by the action of the cricothyroid muscles which tilt the anterior part of the cricoid cartilage cranially and so carry the arytenoid cartilages dorsally (stretching action of the vocal folds).

G. Relaxation of the vocal folds, produced by the action of the thyroarytenoid muscles, which draw the arytenoid cartilages ventrally (downward).[17]

Note especially in Fig. 11 the back (posterior) view of the cricoarytenoid muscles, which primarily control phonation in the upper vocal range. They cause the vocal bands to be adducted in the manner illustrated in Fig. 10.

Fig. 12 shows a view of the larynx from the posterior

42

aspect in a cut-away diagram. Of particular note is the ventricle of Morgagni (laryngeal sinus), the spaces between the vocal folds and the vestibular folds (called the false cords). These ventricular folds are located just above the vocal folds. There exists some dispute as to whether these laryngeal sinus cavities (ventricular chambers) influence amplification of the tone initiated by the vocal bands, thus affecting resonance. Vennard believes that the ventricles are not a resonating chamber,[18] while Appelman regards the area as a potential resonating system, but that their formant contribution to the tonal system is somewhat in doubt at this time.[19]

Fig. 13 shows the various folds and cartilages surrounding the vocal bands as one might peer down the larynx.

THE RESONATORS

After the sound is initiated by the vibrator (vocal folds), it must be amplified and given its tonal character by the resonators. All of the resonators must be well-coordinated with the vibrator, i. e., the correct size and shape of the buccalpharyngeal cavity (mouth and pharynx) must be formed to provide proper amplification for each individual tone on each pitch.

My objective here is to provide a thumbnail sketch of the resonating areas in preparation for further reference in succeeding chapters. However, it is important for any singer or teacher to realize that, according to Vennard, certain principles should be accepted as a basis for understanding resonance in singing, paraphrased as follows:

Any resonator is a secondary vibrator.

43

> The vocal resonator is a column of air and not a
> sounding board of some sort, such as stringed in-
> struments.

> The shape of the resonator is not only complex, but
> highly variable. Thus, it may vibrate as a whole
> or in any of its parts.[20] (See Fig. 1.)

The Trachea (windpipe)

There seems to be little consensus among vocal scientists as to the amount of resonance (if any) that the windpipe has in regard to supporting the sound produced by the
vibrator. Vennard believes, however, that it does act as a
resonator and presents a chart of "Bronchotracheal Resonance" in his book. This chart is a reproduction of van den
Berg's graph first printed in a NATS Bulletin.[21] Some
vocal instructors identify certain qualities of so-called
"chest resonance" with the tracheal area. The trachea's
main function, of course, is to bring air into the lungs.

The Larynx

Vennard opines that the larynx is also a resonator:
"Startling as it may be, our most prized resonance may be
here!"[22] However, there seems to be no empirical evidence
that there is any sensation of resonance, per se, in the
larynx itself for the singer.

The Ventricles

As said earlier in this chapter, Vennard and Appelman
are not in agreement as to whether the ventricles perform
any resonating function. I support the notion that this chamber has some resonating properties. At least we should be
cognizant of its influence in singing.

VOCAL ANATOMY

The Pharynx

This cavity is divided into three sections by vocal scientists: laryngopharynx, oro (oral) pharynx, and nasopharynx. (See Fig. 1, page 25.)

Traditionally, vocal scientists and teachers have recognized the important influence this region has in the proper amplification of tone; that the true timbre of the voice is largely developed in this cavity.

The laryngopharynx (labeled "pharynx" in Fig. 1) is an important resonator in the coupled phonatory system, according to Appelman.

> It extends from the tip of the epiglottis, which covers the lid to the superior surface of the vocal folds; its lateral boundaries are the aryepiglottic folds which completely enfold it. Its superior orifice is the epiglottis, which covers the lid during the act of swallowing.[23]

The size and shape of the oral pharynx is governed primarily by the action of the soft palate and tongue during the production of vowels and consonants.

> The oropharynx is most amenable to change through the movement of the larynx. Its transverse dimension is altered by the action of the pharyngeal constrictor [yawning sensation] muscles and the muscles of articulation.[24]

The nasopharynx does not serve as a primary resonator, according to Appelman, because the production of most vowels and consonants cause the uvula to press firmly against the pharyngeal wall, consequently closing the entrance to the nasopharyngeal area.[25] It serves only as a resonator for the production of nasal consonants "n," "m," and "ng," French nasalized vowels and also when the velum is deliberately pulled forward in singing to achieve a "brighter" vocal sound. I refer to this action as the "forward thrust," which will be described later.

The Soft Palate (velum)

Above and in front of the oral pharynx is the soft palate. It is composed of muscle and tissue extending backward from the hard palate. It has an appendage called the uvula, and as a unit it moves away from the tongue to form the variety of shapes required to form vowels in speech and in singing. (Ventriloquists can manipulate this area to form vowels without moving their jaws or lips appreciably.)

According to Appelman, where the soft palate and uvula are raised (in the slight yawning position required for good vocal production), the velum surface becomes taut and firm, and thus, acts as a reflector of sound. [26]

The Antra (sinus cavities)

Until scientific experiments were conducted recently, the sinus cavities were believed to be important resonators. Vennard's research into this notion involved filling the nasal passages with gauze and the maxillary sinuses with water. The conclusion was that neither "nasal" nor "sinus" "resonance" has validity; that whatever vibration takes place is merely the sensation which the singer experiences. Consequently, these vibrations are not heard by the listener. [27] However, we cannot ignore the fact that certain nasal sounds, such as "m," "n," "ng" (sub-vowels) require the passage of tone to travel through the nasal cavity, because the mouth is closed. Obviously, these sounds are of lower decibels as

a result of the resistance encountered in the nasal tract and
the lack of amplification space. To test this fact, one need
only to close his nose tightly while phonating any of the above
sounds: the tone stops abruptly. Thus, we can conclude
that the nasal cavity has resonance features only when the
mouth is closed and the nose is open.

The Hard Palate (roof of the mouth)

This section of the mouth consists of bony structure
which serves, among other things, to anchor the teeth. Its
relatively hard surface has been regarded traditionally by
vocal instructors as the final focal point of the tone just behind the upper front teeth. However, contemporary vocal
scientists seem to ignore its function as a resonator separate
from the soft palate, for I find no specific reference to the
hard palate in regard to resonance. In my own teaching experience, I have found that when the soft palate is elevated
in singing, it is most helpful for the student to imagine the
vowel (and thus the tone) to be focused "high in the arch"
of the hard palate, just behind the front teeth. For me,
this produces a proper combination of mellowness and brilliance in the tone quality of the singer.

The Oral Cavity

The mouth (buccal cavity) and entire pharynx are directly interrelated to form the buccalpharyngeal cavity--a unit
which provides specific characteristics for the vocal sounds
emitted by the vibrator. The position of the tongue influences
the size and, to some degree, the shape of this cavity (including the lips). The "architectural shape" of the oral

cavity of each individual also influences vocal timbre. In my teaching experience, I have observed that those singers who possess wide palates (broad facial structure), have more difficulty focusing tones on closed vowels, such as OH and OO, than those with narrow palates, particularly in the upper ranges of their voices.

Another anatomical problem of the oral cavity for singers is that of dentures. A former singer-colleague of mine, who had a complete upper dental plate, explained that the timbre of his voice changed markedly after he received his dentures. He explained that, even though he attempted to lift his soft palate and velum in singing or speaking, the hard surface of the denture palate caused his tone quality to be very "brassy." Since that discussion with my colleague, I have noted also that tonal focus is more difficult for persons with dentures. My analysis of this phenomenon is that the dental plate changes the size and shape of the oral cavity as well as substituting a harder surface for the individual's original hard palate. (This phenomenon has been supported in conversation with a practicing dentist.)

The Total Resonating System

While the hard palate cannot make any physical adjustments, one must consider three very important factors which influence the production of sound. First, shapes and sizes vary greatly from mouth to mouth: palates range from very wide and shallow to very high and narrow. Second, the size of the oral opening (mouth) and the thickness of the lips also should be considered in the final shaping of the resonator: one need only to consider carefully these "architectural" differences in order to realize that the "oral acoustical chamber" (size and shape) influences timbre, quality and volume. Third, the position of the tongue--whether it is flat, thick and/or "humped up" in the oral pharynx like a ski slope--greatly hinders resonance.

Thus, proper resonance for a given vowel on a given pitch is governed by a relationship of all the resonating cavities and moving parts of the buccalpharyngeal cavity. There must be a primary resonance from the pharynx and soft palate to provide needed "velvet" fundamental to the tone as it combines with the high partials produced by the nasal areas and hard palate. The latter supplies the brilliance and the carrying power which further embellishes the tone.

The respective roles these resonators play in singing are often governed by the individual's taste. Some teachers and singers prefer a more "pingy, brassy" sound, while others subscribe to a darker, "throaty" tone. To some degree this is a matter of individual taste and innate timbre, but neither extreme (brassy or throaty) can be condoned by any perceptive person. Full-bodied tone is a result of combining these "highs" and "lows."

Therefore, it seems logical to conclude that the size and shape of the buccalpharyngeal cavity, as well as the composition of the tissues of the various resonating areas, govern the quality of the sounds produced by the vibrator. We think of vowels as possessing various "colors" (characteristics), but also, they are the basic means by which we shape the resonators to amplify the tone. The vowels have a variety of formants, some of which reinforce the tones as they pass through the resonating areas.

SINGING

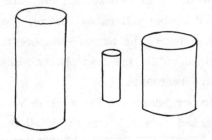

Figure 14, Resonator Illustrations.

An earlier experiment by Redfield still has validity in illustrating the influence exerted upon the vibrator by the resonating cavities. (See Fig. 14.)

Fig. 14 shows examples of varying size resonators which produce varying timbres with the same initial sounds. The quality of the tone produced by such an instrument (mouthpiece plus cylindrical pipe or cavity) is always dependent upon two main factors: the manner in which the generator vibrates and the shape of the resonator.[28]

In recent years, vocal scientists have investigated the concept of vowel formants. This concept deals with the several frequency regions of intensity in a sound spectrum, which combine to determine the characteristic quality of a vowel sound.

> The formant frequencies are determined by the shape of the vocal tract. If the vocal tract were a perfect cylinder closed at the glottis and open at the lips and 17.5 centimeters (about seven inches) long, which is right for the average adult male, then the first four formants would be close to 500, 1500, 2500 and 3500 hertz (cycles per second). Given a longer or shorter vocal tract, these basic frequencies are somewhat lower or higher.... [29]

This passage illustrates the fact that science has developed insights into our consideration of how the voice is produced with optimum results. Yet, it behooves the singers and teachers to use this information in a practical manner. Again, I am led to the conclusion that a clearly defined vowel concept on every pitch throughout the singer's range is the surest way to achieve the proper formants.

In conclusion, it should be helpful to note the views of a variety of scholars in the field of vocal science and speech therapy.

> ... the processes of phonation and resonation are related to each other as cause and effect. The line of demarcation is not clearly made. [30]

The voice pathologist, E. D. Freud states:

> In 'acoustic science' resonance means the prolongation or increase of any sound by reflection. It is the property of sonorous bodies to vibrate in unison with the vibration of other bodies and thus reinforce the original sound. [31]

> The human voice, as we hear it, is the product of two components: first of sound-producing rhythmical air waves, created by the rhythmical movements of the vocal cords, and, second, while passing through the oral and nasal cavities, those rhythmical waves of air, or sound waves, undergo certain modifications, called resonance. [32]

Vennard contributes an important factor for us to consider in singing resonance: the composition of the resonator walls; that is, the softness or hardness of these surfaces influences resonance; that soft walls absorb the rapid, short-wave vibrations making sweeter, more mellow quality, and hard surfaces making the tone more brilliant by reflecting the high partials. [33] Rose states:

51

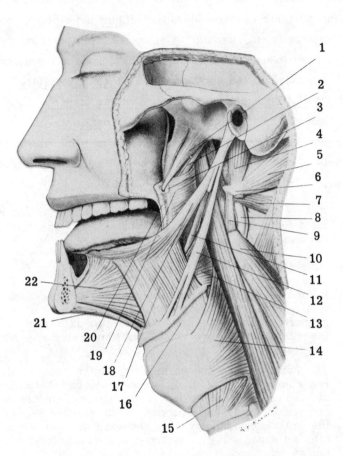

Legend: 1 Tensor veli palatini, 2 Levator veli palatini, 3 Pterygoid hamulus, 4 Rectus capitis lateralis,
5 Superior oblique, 6 Transverse process of atlas,
7 Inferior oblique, 8 Vertebral artery, 9 Anterior
intertransverse, 10 Transverse process of axis, 11
Stylopharyngeus, 12 Stylohyoid, 13 Middle constrictor, 14 Inferior constrictor, 15 Cricothyroid, 16
Thyrohyoid membrane, 17 Hyoglossus, 18 Styloglos-
sus 19 Superior constrictor, 20 Buccinator, 21
Geniohyoid, 22 Genioglossus.

Figure 15, Extrinsic Muscles of the Vocal Mechanism that
Affect Singing. (Reproduced by permission from Gray's
Anatomy, 35th British Edition.)

if the tuning of the vibrator and the resonating system is accurate, i.e., if the pitch of the vibrator and that of the resonating system correspond, we get a marked amplification of the original vibrations. [34]

Since all of the muscles of the vocal mechanism need to be coordinated in the singing process, any buccalpharyngeal tension, quite logically, will restrict efficient production of the sounds begun by the vibrator. In short, buccalpharyngeal tension will restrict the musculature of the vibrator.

> There is more agreement among teachers of singing upon the fact that the pharynx must be as open and free from constrictive tension as possible than upon any other principle of singing. [35]

Lungs

Fig. 16 outlines the respiratory system so that the passages and the "power generator" of action (lungs) can be seen at a glance. (Both lungs are the same, but this illustration indicates separate parts for the sake of clarity.)

The lungs are composed of spongy elastic tissue and are fixed to the lower end of the trachea, and they also house the tiny air sacs, bronchi and blood vessels which supply oxygen to the heart and eventually to the bloodstream. However, in singing and in speaking, they assume the role of the "power supply" for the vibrating mechanism, something other than their primary function was designed to perform.

In singing, an expanded amount of breath is needed, and this in turn, requires definite coordination of this apparatus to fulfill the rhythmic demands of the music. The rib muscles permit the expansion of the thorax (rib cage) in order to accommodate the needs of inhalation, whether it be for

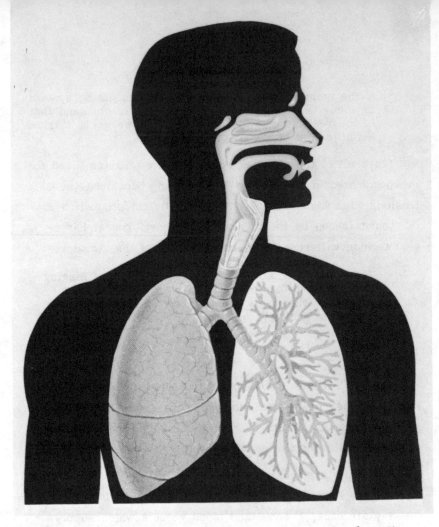

Figure 16, Outline of Respiratory System, showing lung tissue on the left and bronchial tubes on the right. (Courtesy of the Upjohn Company.)

---

singing or replacement of oxygen during and after significant physical exertion.

If the vocal musculature is efficient, the amount of air exhaled is released gradually, and thus, can serve the vocal apparatus for long musical phrases. Breath management also demands superior physical condition and coordination of all of the muscles involved in inhalation and exhalation of breath. Proper posture, combined with good muscle tone and efficient tone production should result in what is traditionally termed good "breath control."

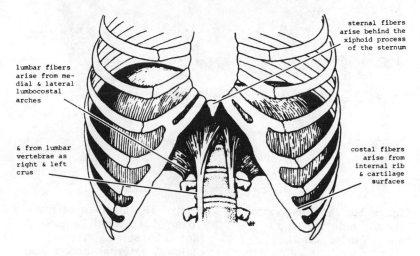

sternal fibers
arise behind the
xiphoid process
of the sternum

lumbar fibers
arise from me-
dial & lateral
lumbocostal
arches

& from lumbar
vertebrae as
right & left
crus

costal fibers
arise from
internal rib
& cartilage
surfaces

Figure 17, the Diaphragm, seen from the front. (Drawing by James J. Van Hare, M.D.)

The diaphragm is a muscular and fibrous partition which separates the thorax from the abdomen. During inhalation, the diaphragm contracts (moves downward), and exerts pressure on the liver, stomach, spleen and intestines causing the front abdominal wall to be pushed outward. The interior pressure of this anterioabdominal "wall" of muscles forces the viscera (internal body organs) and the diaphragm upward. [36]

> This action applies a steady uninterrupted flow of breath pressure against the vocal folds ... [and is] most efficiently utilized when there is no undue tension in the neck and throat. [37]

55

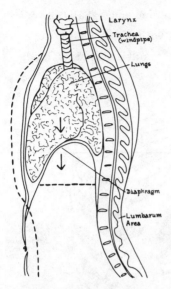

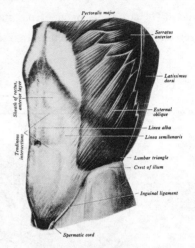

Figure 18, the Respiratory System, side view by Nancy Vander Linde.

Figure 19, Muscles of the Torso that Should Be Employed in Singing; the left obliquus externus abdominis. (Reproduced by permission from Gray's Anatomy, 35th British edition.)

Veins and arteries run through the diaphragm, but its chief function is to control inhalation and exhalation. It contracts by way of a nerve signal from the brain.

Diaphragmatic and costal (rib) action can function independently of each other, proving that the ribs can remain extended, even though the diaphragm moves back upward to its normal curve after exhalation.

Abdominal and Lower Back Muscles

The External oblique, the Linea alba and semilunaris muscles (Fig. 19), the Erector spinae and Quadratus and

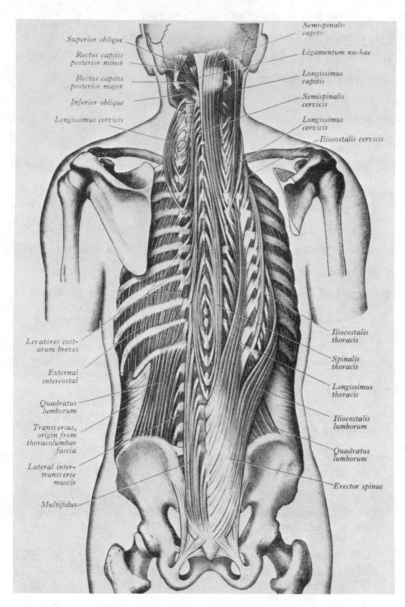

Figure 20, Muscles of the Back that Should Be Employed in Singing. Gray's Anatomy, 35th British ed.

Iliocostalis muscles (Fig. 20) along with the thoracic (rib) muscles constitute the basic musculature which aids in establishing abdominally controlled respiration in singing. A discussion of their function will be presented in Chapter VI.

SUMMARY

When all three areas of the vocal anatomy described above are well-coordinated and developed to maximum capacity, the singer should be able to make progress toward his optimum potential. He should seek to accomplish this goal through systematic practice of music and realistic musical exercises. It should be noted also that good physical condition of the singer is a requisite for good singing, for an inferior musical instrument cannot produce beautiful music.

References

[1] Frederick Husler and Yvonne Rodd-Marling, Singing: The Physical Nature of the Vocal Organ (New York: October House, 1965), p. 17.

[2] Johan Sundberg, "The Acoustics of the Singing Voice," Scientific American 236:3 (March 1977), 82.

[3] Arnold Rose, The Singer and the Voice (New York: St. Martin's Press, 1971), p. 107.

[4] Roger Warwick and Peter Williams, ed., Gray's Anatomy, 35th British ed., (Philadelphia: W. B. Saunders, exclusive distributors, 1973), p. 1173.

[5] R. D. Lockhart; G. F. Hamilton; and F. W. Fyfe, Anatomy of the Human Body (Philadelphia: J. B. Lippincott, 1959), p. 538.

[6] Victor Fields, Foundations of the Singer's Art (New York: Vantage Press, 1977), p. 90.

[7]Ibid., pp. 88-89.

[8]Richard Luchsinger and Godfrey Arnold, Voice--Speech--Language (Belmont, Calif.: Wadsworth Pub. Co., 1965), pp. 25-26.

[9]Fields, Foundations, p. 90.

[10]William Vennard, Singing; The Mechanism and the Technic (New York: Carl Fischer, 1968), p. 39.

[11]Cornelius Reid, Voice: Psyche and Soma (New York: Joseph Patelson Music House, 1975), p. 42.

[12]Luchsinger and Arnold, Voice, p. 14.

[13]Rose, The Singer, pp. 110-111.

[14]Friedrich Brodnitz, Keep Your Voice Healthy (New York: Harper Bros., 1953), plate between pp. 16-17.

[15]D. Ralph Appelman, The Science of Vocal Pedagogy (Bloomington: Indiana University Press, 1967), p. 69.

[16]Fields, Foundations, p. 189-190.

[17]Gray's Anatomy, p. 1181.

[18]Vennard, Singing, p. 90.

[19]Appelman, The Science, p. 77.

[20]Vennard, Singing, p. 82.

[21]Ibid., p. 87.

[22]Ibid., p. 89.

[23]Appelman, The Science, p. 77.

[24]Ibid.

[25]Ibid.

[26]Ibid.

[27]Vennard, Singing, p. 94-96.

[28]John Redfield, Music; A Science and an Art (New York: Tudor, 1935), p. 267.

[29]Sundberg, "The Acoustics," p. 83.

[30]Victor Fields, Training the Singing Voice (New York: King's Crown Press, 1947), p. 144.

[31]E. D. Freud, "Voice Pathology and the Emergence of a New Vocal Style," Archives of Otolaryngology 62 (1955), 51.

[32]Ibid.

[33]Vennard, Singing, pp. 84-85.

[34]Rose, The Singer, pp. 56-57.

[35]Vennard, Singing, p. 92.

[36]Emilio Agostoni, "Action of the Respiratory Muscles," Respiration, vol. I, Sec. III Handbook of Physiology, (Washington, D.C.: American Physiological Society, 1964), p. 378 (as quoted by Appelman, The Science, p. 13).

[37]Appelman, The Science, p. 13.

CHAPTER III

THE VOWEL SPECTRUM:
ITS APPLICATION TO SINGING

This chapter embraces the concept that tone production
is based upon vowel production; that good voweling produces
improved tone quality; that bad voweling produces inferior
tone quality. There is no other means by which color,
character and variety are given to speech or singing than
through vowel formation. The singer's tone quality (rich,
full or sonorous; muddy, thick or dull; thin, nasal or "dead")
is directly related to the way in which the oral pharynx and
tongue are shaped. One does not produce tones completely
independent of words; rather, one utilizes words (language)
as the primary means of producing sounds which should be
intelligible to the listener. Words also provide structure
and give clues to the interpretive aspects of a song.

Singing Is Sustained Speech

One mode of stating this approach to singing is found in
my theory that singing is an extension of speech--the sustaining of spoken sounds which are identified with a wide range
of specific pitches. Obviously, the singing range contains a
vastly greater compass of pitches than does the speaking
voice. Moreover, the act of singing requires accurate identification with various notes of the scale. These differences
between singing and speech production are those of duration

and compass; yet, the basic process of phonation and characterization of sound remains essentially the same in both idioms. Therefore, proper vowel production must be utilized constantly in speech and in singing in order to gain maximum efficiency from the sound-producing mechanism.

To support these assumptions, I wish to quote some vocal authorities:

> Actually, every vibrator adjustment includes an appropriate resonator adjustment. And the vowel is the chief factor whereby this dual adjustment, this coupling system, is secured.[1]

> If the cavity is right, the sound will be right.... The perfect cavity makes the perfect vowel.[2]

> So many people have developed faulty speech habits that their natural singing voices, if they had any, have been affected.[3]

> Voice is speech, and is produced by the mouth [buccalpharyngeal cavity], not by the vocal cords. The vocal cords produce only sounds, [really "puffs"] which are transformed into vowels and consonants by a phonetic process taking place in the mouth, and giving origin to the voice.[4]

> ... [M]ost of the failures in the singing profession are due to the ignorance of the important role played by the speaking voice in relation to the art of singing.[5]

If one can accept the premise that the vowel in singing is the basis of tone production, then it is also logical to conclude that every vowel has its unique size and shape on every given pitch and dynamic level (however subtle the change may be for notes that are a half or a whole step apart); that the most reliable clue to the shape of a given sound (not necessarily size, as will be explained later) is gained through the concept of speech. An excellent singing practice is to carefully pronounce (speak) a word that is to

be sung, observing in a mirror one's mouth shape and size;
then sing it immediately, in a comfortable middle range of
the voice at mezzoforte dynamic, being certain to add the
correct buccalpharyngeal depth required by the height of the
pitch. That is to say, that there must be enough "lift of
the soft palate" or slight yawning feeling in the oral pharynx
to add depth to the tone. However, this addition of depth
must always be within the confines of the correct vowel focus.
The basic vowel focus must never be distorted by being too
large, too small, and/or malformed. For instance, many
singers pronounce the word "heaven" as "haahven" instead
of "hehven"--an obvious distortion of the word. The buccalpharyngeal cavity must be accurately formed as it is combined with just enough arching of the soft palate (velum) to
provide the proper tonal formant. Also, the tone (vowel)
must be focused narrowly in the mask in order to distinguish
the "eh" from the wider "aah" vowel sound. In other words,
the "eh" vowel has a narrower shape than the "aah" vowel.
(See "Vowel Derivations" in Vowel Spectrum, page 69.)

Even though the tone is considerably more sustained in
singing than in speech, the fact that good singing is an extension or expansion of the basic principles of good speech, suggests that the vocalist should attempt to develop the best possible speech habits. Slovenly speech leads to weak and diffused vocal production in many cases, although it is true
that some singers, who speak poorly, employ stronger vowel
production in singing. However, I maintain that the most
natural approach to singing is through the development of
good speech habits. The sounds which one "speaks" during
the act of singing should be articulated with great accuracy
(vowel focus) to achieve both clarity of production as well
as to maintain tonal vitality.

63

To summarize, the basic differences between good singing and good speaking practices are that:

> Singing requires specific pitches and a wider range of
> sounds than in speaking.

> Singing requires arbitrary lengths of time spent on
> certain vowel sounds (because of specific note values),
> whereas in speech many sounds can be dropped or
> "thrown away," such as "er" (uhr) as in "never,"
> "ih" as in "divine," "y" (EE) as in "glory," "ih" as
> in "hear" and the modified "ah" as in "affection."
> (See Vowel Spectrum, p. 69.)

> Proper singing employs vibrato.

The Italian Language

It cannot be over-emphasized that the Italian language is
the purest and most singable of all of our modern European
languages.   Historically, the Italian people have produced a
larger percentage of noted solo singers than any other country in the world (although this is not so true of contemporary
Italy, because of the preoccupation with political and economic
survival).   The basic reason for this phenomenon is the
Italian language.   Most vocal authorities agree that the language best suited to consistently good tone production in
singing is properly spoken Italian, because of its basic simplicity and its pure vowels.   Some of the most respected
teachers of all time were the first bel canto teachers, such
as Caccini, 1558-1615, Tosi, 1656-1732, Porpora, 1686-1766,
Vaccai, 1790-1848, and Concone, 1810-1861.   (Vaccai and
Concone vocalises are still used by some contemporary voice
teachers.)   The following is the opinion of Lilli Lehmann,
one of the most famous and gifted singers of all time:

> Without doubt the Italian language, with its wealth of

vowels, is better adapted for singing than the German language, so rich in consonants, or any other language.[6]

Contrast the pure Italian vowels to those of the French language with its many vowel shadings, nuances and nasal sounds: ideally, the French vowels must be modified to resemble the Italian vowels if consistently good vocal production is to be achieved. The shape of the "horn," then, greatly influences the amplification and resonance of the sound waves produced by the vibrating cords; the amplifier must reinforce the sounds produced by the vibrator (see page 25). It is also customary for singers performing in any language to use the Italian "r" (rolled or flipped with the tip of the tongue) rather than, for instance, the German gutteral "r," the French constricted "r," or the hard English-American "r." The Italian "r" sound eliminates tongue tension found in most Western European languages. Of course, there are instances in which the tongue is not flipped in singing, especially in English: soft endings in which the tone diminishes or in words which are not declamatory in nature.

The Principle of the "Aural Image"

A safe generalization to make is that the mind must direct the vocal musculature to form the desired vocal pitch. The mind also must envision the aural image (the character of the sound: loud, soft; firm, gentle; etc.) before the sound is produced by the vibrator. An actor must imagine (subconsciously, at least) the manner in which he will speak a given line before he can deliver it. People who "can't act" simply cannot "hear" or imagine in advance the aural image--the manner in which to speak their lines. Likewise, the singer must simultaneously imagine both the pitch and the tone color of what he is "speaking" on the vocal pitches in order to give adequate expression (characterization) to the musical and vocal efforts. Since the actor or speaker must envision the tone color of what he is about to say, the same principle applies to the vocalist, because singing is an extension of speech. This is precisely why it is so very important that the singing student and the singing teacher recognize the value of the aural image.

One of the standard practices in vocal pedagogy is for the teacher to sing a note or phrase and ask the student to imitate it. This custom is frequently successful for the advanced singer, or for the teacher to illustrate an interpretive point, but something more tangible is needed to aid the average student in achieving better tone production than rote response to the teacher's example.

In order to attain this objective, the singer should have additional guidance to help him identify as well as produce the desired tone quality. A danger in the use of imitation is that the singer cannot hear his own voice as others hear it. Thus, it is extremely easy for the singer to err in ascertaining what constitutes good sound. (One of the greatest aids to vocal pedagogy today is the tape recorder. A tape machine of good quality can be of great value in helping the singer to associate the external sounds others hear with the internal sounds he hears during the act of singing.) The vehicle through which the voice student can gain insight into his vocal production is a concise understanding of vowel production. The following quote supports this contention that

there must exist a proper shaping between the oral pharynx
and the tongue:

> [E]ach fundamental [tone] is associated with a series
> of overtones. It is the accentuation of certain
> brands of these overtones which produces what is
> called the 'vowel sound.' The term 'vowel' is,
> then, a special case of 'quality' or 'timbre' in
> which certain groups of harmonies [harmonics] are
> either accentuated or suppressed by means of
> shaping the adjustable cavities[7] [emphasis added].

With the vowel specifically identified as the basis for
clear sound production and the Italian language established
as the ideal vowel sounds to emulate, the following Vowel
Spectrum is presented. The chart is arranged to show the
relationships between the English and the basic Italian vowel
sounds and their application to singing. The Vowel Spectrum
is the heart of my approach to singing and my teaching of
the art. It is also a "stencil" for pronunciation in singing
in many languages.

Luchsinger and Arnold use a similar term to describe the process which amplifies and gives character to
the sound vibrations produced in the larynx.

> As soon as the sound mixture, produced in the
> laryngeal generator ... is led to the coupled sys-
> tem of the pharyngeal and oral cavities, one can
> predict ... how the sound spectrum will be altered
> in the resonating tube.... The configuration of
> the coupled resonating spaces may be voluntarily
> changed, within certain limits, by the articulatory
> positioning of the oral chamber[8] [emphasis added].

I interpret this to say that the size and shape of the buccalpharyngeal cavity governs both the amplification and the tone
quality of the voice.

Sundberg also refers to the "spectrum of a sung vowel"
in his discussion of vowel formants.[9]

In employing the Vowel Spectrum the five basic Italian vowels are aligned with the comparable five English vowels using the English pronunciation according to the <u>American Heritage Dictionary</u>, 1973 edition. The vowel sounds are identified as they relate to the <u>core</u> of the sound as opposed to the IPA (International Phonetic Alphabet), which deals with combining sounds as in diphthongs or identifying them with the many confusing symbols of that alphabet. In essence the Vowel Spectrum is a simplified and clear presentation of phonics as applied to singing. The symbols cited on the chart (page 69) indicate how we should pronounce the words when singing in English, and they are only a small sample of examples found in our language. However, the Vowel Spectrum can be applied successfully to most other languages. (Examples are in the Appendix.)

One further admonition to be emphasized here is that our English orthography frequently bears little relation to our phonology and thus it behooves us in this study always to keep in mind the vowel sound which is to be articulated, rather than the actual spelling of the word.

It is to be asserted again that the IPA, as employed in singing, tends to inhibit the singer, because it is too precise and too complicated to apply to instinctive, artistic singing. (The IPA is a valuable tool in the study of languages; even so, one of its strong supporters, D. Ralph Appelman, in his thorough treatise, <u>The Science of Vocal Pedagogy</u>, also admits that "phonetic analysis is a hopeless task, for if one listens closely enough to any word that is uttered, the number of different features one can find is endless."[10] The Vowel Spectrum more naturally permits the "different features" of language pronunciation to be adapted

68

THE VOWEL SPECTRUM

PRINCIPAL VOWELS

Basic Italian	i	e	a	o	u
Basic English	EE	AY	AH	OH	OO
Examples:	see	say	sight (AH-ee)	so	soon
	dream	fail	father	hold	too, ruler
	seize, grieve	save	star, heart	mow, sew	rude
	believe	late	on, odd	goal	you (ee-OO)
	reach	they, pray	ice (AH-ee)	soul	blew, blue
	real	praise	thou (AH-oo)	omit, obey	rebuke (ee-OO)

VOWEL DERIVATIONS

	ih	eh	aah	aw	uuh	uhr ♭
Examples:	sit, myth, guilt	set, wed, head	sat, hand, and	sought, saw	soot, should	serve, her
	women, weary	guest, yes	shadow	God (some prefer "ah")	could, full	fur, work
	pretty, busy	bury, any	man, can	warm	good, book	learn, term
	fill, live	said	had, glad	all, hall	crooked	world, word
	hear, fear	their	rapture	ought, naught	startled	over, bird
	kingdom	prepared	that	walk, water	put, stood	mercy

SUB-VOWELS (consonants that sustain pitches)

m, n, (ng), l, r (uhr--above), v, z

MODIFIED VOWELS

	ah†	"ah" ɐ	"oh" (open Italian "o")
Examples:	mother, come, one	the, a, sofa	Lord, yore, glory, for
	of, love, suffers	idea, but, cut	morn, mourn, adore
	blood, wonder	cup, circus	oil (oh-ih-l), boy (oh-ee)

†Three forms of the "a" vowel: AH as in father, ah as in mother and "ah" as in the (see page 21).
♭This sound replaces the [ɜ] of the IPA. ♯Replaces [ə] and [ʌ] of the IPA.

to the singing process, although some speech sounds found
in various geographical locations of almost any country may
be unacceptable for what the Western world considers to be
good voice production: South German Schwäbische, even
some areas of Italy, the Southeastern United States, the
Midwestern hard and flat sounds, etc.) The straight-forward
application of vowel sounds, as illustrated in the Vowel
Spectrum, page 69, frees the singer to develop and maintain
a subconscious--yet precise--aural image of the correct
vowel and tone color which he should produce.

Careful examination of the Vowel Spectrum underscores
the fact that many of our English vowels really sound the
same in pronunciation, even though the spelling is different
and many words, spelled differently, sound the same. Cog-
nizance of the existence of homonyms will prove to be of
significant aid to the singer in forming the correct aural
image of the vowel (vocal) sound which he or she should
produce. It is vitally important in the application of this
system of vocal pedagogy that the singer identify every
sound he produces with this simplified concept of the vowel.

Diphthongs

Diphthongs "AY" + "EE" (as in "say"), "AH" +
"EE" (as in "sight") and "OH" + "oo" (as in "so") should
be treated carefully so as not to combine the sounds in
singing. The principal sound (always the first of the two
vowels in English diphthongs except for our English vowel
U [ee-OO]) should be held until the end of the note-duration,
when it unites with the consonant (if any) ending the word;
the last half of the diphthong acts in place of the consonant,

70

such as in "pray" (AY + ee) or "go" (OH + oo). (Treatment of diphthongs will be discussed in more detail on pages
99-100.) The second sound may be considered to be a vanishing sound, although it must always be clearly articulated in
order to maintain intensity of the tone and the identity of
the word. In short, one should sing on the center of the
vowel just as one should sing on the center of the pitch.

Modified Vowels

The modified vowels are directly related to the major
vowels "AH" and "OH" and should be considered basically
the same as the principal vowel sounds, except that these
modified sounds are not quite as deeply-set (as large in size)
as the principal vowel sounds. In forming these modified
vowels during speech, one can easily discern that the basic
difference between modified and principal vowels is the duration of the modulated speech sounds. In singing, the duration
of the note dictates the length of time to be spent on the
various vowel sounds, whereas, in speaking, a vanishing
vowel is often "thrown away." Hence, in singing, we must
usually assign arbitrary lengths of time to the particular
vowel sounds, despite their shorter duration in speaking.
This is the source of the theory that singing is an extension
of speech. Therefore, deepening the modified vowels to
resemble the principal vowels, from which they are derived,
improves resonance and focus of these otherwise less resonant sounds. (See Vowel Spectrum for examples.)

Application of the Vowel Spectrum Toward Tonal Focus

Pronounce (speak) the vowel sounds in order (below),

71

being careful to <u>sustain</u> <u>the</u> <u>sounds</u> and <u>segue</u> from one to
the other. Note that "EE" is relatively small in size; "AY"
is larger, and "AH" is the largest; then "OH" is smaller
again and "OO" is still smaller, about the same size (but
not the same shape) as "EE." Also note that the English
diphthong "AY" moves back to "EE" and the diphthong "OH"
moves to "OO." Consequently, <u>it</u> <u>is</u> <u>imperative</u> <u>that</u> <u>the</u>
<u>singer</u> <u>refrain</u> <u>from</u> <u>mixing</u> <u>these</u> <u>sounds</u> (vowel migration)
<u>when</u> <u>sustaining</u> <u>a</u> <u>note</u> <u>on</u> <u>any</u> <u>of</u> <u>these</u> <u>vowels.</u> This avoids
muddy voweling and bad diction.

The feeling should be:

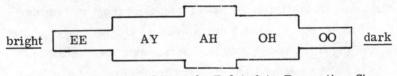

bright   EE   AY   AH   OH   OO   dark

Figure 21, Principal Vowels Related to Respective Size

The diphthong "OY" ("oh" + ee), as in the word
"boy," should be cited as a potential problem vowel sound.
It consists of the modified "oh" (open Italian "O") and the
vanishing "ee" sounds (see Vowel Spectrum under Modified
Vowel "oh").

If the singer fully understands these relationships, he
should have a clue to the <u>basic</u> shapes and sizes of the vowels
as they relate to singing, especially in the middle and lower
areas of his or her voice.

"AH" is the center or "neutral" sound, and the other
vowel sounds surround and relate to it. Note also, that if
one forms "EE" or "OO" with the same amount of space in
the buccalpharyngeal cavity as "AH" on the same set of
pitches, he will produce an over-sized vowel formation on

these smaller vowels. This malformation prevents good
vowel focus, the result being a "throaty," dark tone. Singing in this fashion would be somewhat like speaking over a
yawn, only not as extreme. (One cannot speak clearly over
a full yawn. Why do many singers think that an almost full
yawning position of the oral pharynx is the correct one for
singing?) True, there must be some lift of the soft palate
(slight yawn), but it must always be only enough to add the
necessary depth of tone within the focus of the vowel. (Experiment: sing an "AH" vowel, as in "father" and then segue
directly into the "OO" and "EE" vowels while you maintain
the space of the original "AH" sound. You will observe that
the tone is throaty and dull, because these two small vowels
are over-formed (over-sized), or because the tongue is being
held down in the "AH" position, which is too large. (See
Fig. 21.)

There are three distinct vowel sounds to be found in
the "AH family." I catalogue these sounds as the "three
bears": the "father AH", the "mother ah" and the "baby
ah" (see Vowel Spectrum for modified "AH" vowels). They
are best distinguished from each other by their length of duration and, consequently, their depth. The "father AH" is
deep and sounds like the full Italian AH. This form of the
"AH" vowel also includes diphthongs, such as "might,"
"sight," "light," etc. The "mother" ah is less deep and is
of shorter duration when spoken, as in "come," "some,"
and "mother." Finally, the "ah" in our English language
articles a or the are of very short duration. In speech they
become a very dull "uh" sound. Consequently, in order to
obtain optimal tone quality in singing, these shorter ah
sounds (as in "mother" and "the") need to "move toward"

73

the "father AH" in order to achieve proper depth of tone production.   This depth provides enough space in the buccalpharyngeal cavity to produce a more acceptable tone because
this larger "AH" vowel elevates the soft palate to some degree.   This "AH, " combined with a concave (spoon-shaped)
curvature of the tongue, allows ample space for the tone to
be amplified.   (Because of hereditary factors, not all singers
can create a grooved tongue position.   I have discovered in
my teaching experience that those who can do so seem to
have an easier time forming a well-focused tone.)

        The reason for beginning the sequence of vowels with
"EE" is that this "forward-placed" vowel tends to maintain
a brighter sound, particularly needed as the voice ascends
to the upper part of its range.

        The jaw, of course, must be free of tension, "hang-
ing" as though in an imaginary elastic sling.   The jaw should
merely "float, " while the vowel focus is "forward" in the
mask, so to speak.   The jaw should never be jammed open.
It should be noted that jaw tension shows up rather clearly
on "EE" and "OO" vowels, particularly on higher pitches.
A tight jaw also prevents the singer from making the correct
adjustments in the vocal musculature (see Fig. 15).   This
jaw rigidity, in turn, causes the entire vocal musculature to
become rigid, preventing use of the "head voice" in the upper
range.   Consequently, the "EE" and "OO" vowels may be
used in vocalizing with the Vowel Spectrum to identify jaw
tension.

        In a sense, one can say that "speaking" the tone
while singing is insurance against the "woofy, " dark tone.
This concept aids in preventing an over-sized vowel formation.

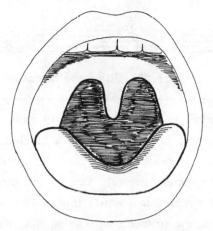

Figure 22, Tongue Position for the "AH" vowel (i.e., released from tension)

A vocalise which I have found helpful in attaining a sense of focus on malformed vowels (such as spreading the tone on large interval skips) is to ask the student to sing octave glissandos (or fifths, or any interval that is presenting the problem) on that particular vowel. Then, have the student imagine a <u>narrow channel</u> that "projects forward" as he ascends to the top of the interval and down again.

When performing the exercise in Fig. 23, the singer should be very careful to <u>hold the vowel focus</u> as he ascends to the high note. Even though he must "open up" to some degree (arching the soft palate slightly) for the rise in pitch, he must always <u>maintain the central focal point of the vowel</u> with which he began singing on the lower note. The student should also be cautioned to keep the vowel focus in the narrow, imaginary channel as he ascends the scale being certain to "project" the tone forward by applying a slight "snarl" or "sneer" so that the upper front teeth show. (Many teachers

Figure 23, Glissando Vocalise

---

advise the student to smile, in order to gain a "forward focus." While this does accomplish a brighter vocal production, I find that the tone also tends to spread--inviting a shallow, less focused tone.) One of my students coined the term "tall vowels" to identify the narrow vowel.

This concept prevents spreading the vowel, and thus the tone, avoiding the "wide open" (blatant) sound. Vowel distortion or lack of focus produces overtones (vowel formants) unsympathetic to the fundamental vibration.

Inaccurate voweling leads to poor blend and intonation in ensemble singing, i.e., when there occurs great variance among the overtones produced by the singers in the group. One might consider the nozzle of a hose to be analogous to tonal focus in that the nozzle projects (focuses) the stream of water that would otherwise have little carrying power. The correct vowel size and shape is the "nozzle" for the sound emanating from the vibrator. This illustrates the effect and underscores the importance which vowel size and shape has upon varying pitches produced by the singer.

Further Use of the Vowel Spectrum

As stated earlier, many singers develop great facility in vocalizing throughout the compass of their voices, and yet cannot adapt their technique adequately to the singing of a song with consistently good tone production and musical expression.

76

VOWEL SPECTRUM

Use of the Vowel Spectrum as a "warm-up" for vocal students and choral groups is especially effective during early stages of exposure to this system of vocal pedagogy. Later, when the principle of the clearly defined, narrow-channeled and deeply-set vowel is mastered, the exercise in Fig. 24 is not a prerequisite for singing (although for some of my students, it is a very reliable mental and vocal "conditioner" before beginning a song). The clearly defined, deeply-set vowel applied to a hymn, chorale or any simple melody accomplishes the same objective of attaining depth and focus of tone.

This vocalise should begin in the singer's lower or middle range. The scale is ascended by half-steps, completing the sequence of the five principal vowels and/or the five vowel derivations on each pitch. (See Fig. 24.) Each singer ascends the scale up to his individual, maximum capacity. The singer(s) should be reminded to form a little "arch" (a slight yawn) with the soft palate, and at the same time should be reminded to "speak" the vowel sound clearly. It must be impressed upon the student that the increase of the arch of the palate is very slight (almost imperceptible) for each higher note of a half or whole degree. The depth of the vowel determines the depth of the tone. The vowel must be "deeply-set" and narrow (not spread and wide), and the projection must be very forward. Attaining this forward projection can be achieved by concentrating upon the vowel focus as being just behind the upper front teeth. It is as though the singer were imagining that he is "hanging" the tone (or vowel pronunciation) on his upper front teeth and gums--while yet keeping the vowel focus clearly in mind.

77

Another thought-process that aids in attaining this
"forward feeling" is that of biting an imaginary apple, while
simultaneously retaining the narrow, deeply-set vowel.
(Note how the upper lip lifts and the projection is unmistak-
ably forward.) This "apple-biting" exercise is particularly
useful with the vowels "EE," "AY," "AH" and "ih," "eh,"
"aah" and "aw"; by contrast, the vowels "OH," "OO," "uuh"
and "uhr" are produced farther back in the throat, and thus
become overformed when the lips are opened to that extent.
However, it is important to caution that the lips should not
be drawn down over the front teeth on these "darker" vowels
lest rigidity occur in the lip muscles. Rather, the lips
should remain flexible and free with the feeling that they
are an integral part of these vowel formations and that they
should be used to "round off" the final phase of the vowel.
In Fig. 24 one may add an "m" before each vowel "mee,
may, mah, moh, moo" to relieve tension in the oral pharynx,
or one also might add a consonant with the principal vowels
(SEE, SAY, SIGHT, SO, SOON) and with the vowel derivations (sit, set, sat, sought, soot) as illustrated on page 79.

The reason for beginning this vocalise in the lower or
middle ranges of the voice is that it is easier for singers
to produce natural vowel sounds at these pitch levels than
at either extreme of their range. (This is particularly true
for unskilled singers.) By vocalizing in a comfortable
range, the unskilled singer (or an experienced one with such
problems as forcing the tones, breathiness, muddy diction,
etc.) can concentrate more effectively upon the relationship
between vowel formation and vocal production.

EE AY AH OH OO EE AY AH OH OO SEE SAY SIGHT SO SOON †
ih eh aah aw uuh ih eh aah aw uuh sit set sat sought soot

†A sequence of words is suggested after the student feels comfortable with the isolated vowels.

Figure 24, Vocalise Applied to the Vowel Spectrum.

The Vowel Spectrum Adaptation for Choral Groups

Chord progressions may be applied to this vocalization on the Vowel Spectrum. This practice may be especially helpful for unison singing in studio class voice lessons or when a choral group vocalizes in unison. However, a cappella singing affords an excellent opportunity for listening to blend and intonation as well as tone production. Other harmonic sequences can be applied to the Vowel Spectrum in order to provide opportunities for developing careful listening habits. The following is only one example of how such a progression might be adapted to this concept:

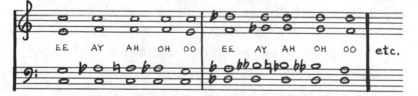

EE   AY   AH   OH   OO   EE   AY   AH   OH   OO   etc.

Figure 25, Vocalise Harmonization of Vowel Spectrum.

The chordal sequence in Fig. 25 is particularly useful with mixed choirs at an early level of vocal study because, in each section, it tends to keep the voices within a comfortable singing range. The singers should be cautioned

79

to minimize the change between vowel sounds as they proceed. In other words, there should be no closures between the sounds during the progression of these vowels. Neophytes tend to envision too much change from EE to AY to AH by inserting a "y" sound between each of these vowels (EE-YAY-YAH-YOH-YOU.)

The choral director should caution the singers to pronounce the vowel sounds with only as much "yawn" as is needed for the desired depth of tone. Simultaneously, he or she should insist upon clear, accurate pronunciation (formation) of the vowels. The latter is most important in order to insure that the vocal sound not become "muddy" or "woofy," and that good diction habits be established. "A singer should have an aural conception of the tone he desires to produce."[11]

Opening the Mouth

It is often difficult to convey to the tyro singer that there must be a slight yawning sensation in singing; that the oral pharynx must have enough "lift" or rise of the soft palate to accommodate a "deeply-set" vowel. Wilson suggests an effective means of dramatizing the need for this space: "Place the [tips of the] first two fingers ... between the teeth with the second (or middle) finger on top."[12]

It is vitally important, however, to warn the singer(s) that, while opening the mouth as widely and deeply as the two fingers dictate, there also must be a conscious effort to keep the tongue from drawing too far back in the oral pharynx. It is difficult to attain tonal clarity with two fingers in the mouth (even though they must be placed so that only the finger tips touch the teeth), but the point is illustrated clearly that there must be ample space in the buccalpharyngeal cavity to amplify adequately the tone produced by the vibrator. As soon as the individual or ensemble members have experienced the need for this "lift of the palate," the use of this drastic "finger technique" should be abandoned and accurate vowel formation be applied to the "space sensation" so as to avoid "muddiness" or "darkness" of tone. "Darkness" should never be confused with depth of tone, for a tone can be sung deeply and clearly without being "dark" in "color."

The buccalpharyngeal cavity changes in size and shape with various vowels and consonants, thus affecting the vowel formants on respective pitches. The areas causing these changes in size and shape of the vocal tract are the soft palate, jaw, tongue and lips. The tongue has many optional positions in singing (or speaking) which may alter the vowel formants. These deviations in shape and size among the various component parts of the buccalpharyngeal cavity cause the shifts in vowel quality. Nevertheless, the core of the vowel sound to be produced must remain vivid in the singer's mind throughout the compass of his total range.

The "Vowel Derivations"

Among the English language vowels there are several sounds which are derived from the principal vowels. These are labeled vowel derivations and are "midway between" the five principal vowels. (See Vowel Spectrum, page 69.) The derivations are:

"ih" as in "sit" (care must be taken to elevate the soft palate "behind" the exact vowel focus)

"eh" as in "set"

"aah" as in "sat" (frequently confused with "AH") †

"aw" as in "sought" (also frequently confused with "AH")

"uuh" as in "soot" (the short form of "OO")

"uhr" as in "serve" (basically "uuh" with only a "leaning" toward "r")

†When "aah" (as in "sat") is sung as "AH," diction also suffers. The "aah" vowel can sustain a tone as acceptable and beautiful as any other, providing it is deeply-set and is the right size and shape for the pitch being sung. There is absolutely no justification for such vowel substitution. Merely adding pharyngeal space will mellow the tone color.

Those persons who rely upon the IPA for vowel pronunciation may feel that these designations are not precise enough. However, that is the main point of the Vowel Spectrum; namely, to eliminate these minute IPA symbols, which, in my teaching experience, are often confusing to the student as he or she tries to envision the natural shaping of the vowel which should be produced on a given pitch.

If the reader will pronounce carefully and slowly all the above vowel sounds in a sustained manner, he will note the relationships between them:

```
     EE     AY     AH     OH     OO
    / \    / \    / \    / \    / \
  ih   eh   aah   aw   uuh   uhr
```

Figure 26, Relationship of Principal Vowels to Vowel Derivations.

In Fig. 26, "ih" is placed first in the sequence because its formation and feel is narrower than "EE." This vowel also needs to be very narrowly arched in order to achieve proper focus. Otherwise "ih" and "eh" will tend to sound alike. This appears to be in contradiction to Appelman's radiograph findings[13] but in my pedagogical experiences this sequence is the most logical way in which the student can differentiate among these sounds as he strives to attain the correct aural image of the respective vowels in the Vowel Spectrum. Also "uhr" is listed both as a vowel derivative and a sub-vowel. That is because the buccal formation for the English letter "r" becomes like that for "uhr" in singing (just "tipping" the "uhh" sound toward the "r"), thus slightly resembling the formation to produce the German umlaut [ü]. Thus, I have assigned it a dual role as a sub-vowel, because it has liquid consonant qualities, as well as those of a vowel derivative, and also since it contains a mixture of vowel sounds that we are forced to pronounce in the English language.

Relating the Vowel Derivatives

It should be emphasized again that "ih" as in "sit" is formed by a very narrow shape of the oral pharynx and lips. It is the most malformed vowel of any in the spectrum. It is often mistaken for "eh," particularly as the singer ascends the scale; "with" is often pronounced as "weth" or even "waath" (a typical example of "spreading the vowel"). Many tenors, as they sing across the passaggio (break), e, f, and g above middle C, emit a blatant, "wide-open" tone because of a shallow formation (mispronunciation) of these vowel derivatives, especially "ih, eh," and "aah." The correct mental image of the basic vowel pronunciation, combined with proper space in the oral pharynx, produces a natural "cover" to the tone. When the singer pronounces "God" as "Gud" ("uh"), the tongue tends to recede in order to compensate for or attempt to synthesize the correct vowel formation. The natural pronunciation of "aw," with a low tongue position produces the correct shape for the diction to be recognizable. (Some people prefer the "AH" sound for "God." Regardless of which sound the singer prefers, the vowel must be clearly defined in his or her mind. Ensemble singers, however, must agree on one or the other pronunciation to achieve good blend.) Again, it should be stressed that malformation of the vowel leads to muscular tension (and vice versa), and that this distortion of the resonator (usually the spreading of the vowel) is the central cause of the singer's poor tone production. Vowel distortion is often caused by ignorance of the fact that many English words, though spelled differently (homonyms), have the same vowel sound. For instance, the words "fear" and "live" are both "ih" vowels. The practice of some teachers is to advise the student to form a darkened "ee" for singing pronunciation of this vowel. This invariably leads to tongue tension--besides the fact that it "muddies" the diction.

Correct vowel pronunciation emanating from precise speech formation, and combined with proper depth, eliminates the need for vocal teachers to tell their students that in order to bridge the so-called "break(s)" in the voice, they should "cover" or "darken" the tone quality. (The term "cover" is a misleading term and should be avoided--especially with beginning students. This will be discussed in more detail later.) For instance, the "AH" vowel should never be pronounced "uh" (the short, dull "ah" form as in the word "up") in order to sing across the passaggio. Rather, the clearly defined "AH" vowel sound should be in the singer's mind with the forward focus behind the upper front teeth. The "snarl" or "sneer" should be coupled with the right amount of lift of the soft palate (beginning of the yawn) to provide the proper relationships of high and low partials. This action will secure the proper formants on the respective vowel sounds and eliminate the heavy "chest voice" production caused by a dull vowel. The singer must experiment to find the right relationship of "snarl" and lift of the soft palate. When the vocal production becomes more free and less labored, the singer has gained insight into his goal of passaggio transition.

If the reader pronounces slowly from left to right through the Vowel Spectrum, he will note that "eh" is midway between "EE" and "AY"; "aah" is between "AY" and "AH, " and so forth. These relationships are helpful avenues to correct vowel production. (See Fig. 26.)

When the singer develops the skill to define clearly in his own mind each of these sounds as they relate to words in the text of the song he is singing, he is aided in producing consistently better tones. This is the all-important aural image about which I have remarked repeatedly. Absence of this mental model of the tone (vowel) inhibits well-focused tone production. To be emphasized again: the singer should form the vowel sound and arch his soft palate simultaneously in relation to the height of the pitch. The oral pharynx should become progressively larger as the scale is ascended. However, vocalists should be cautioned not to spread the vowel by opening the mouth too widely. The arch should be narrow and forward. Also, the oral pharynx should not be elevated (stretched) so much that undue tension or vowel distortion occurs. When the singer forms the proper vowel sound, he will tend also to shape the resonating cavity more accurately to fit the particular pitch he is singing.

Vowel Diffusion ("Losing" the Vowel)

It is important to call attention to the fact that most singers tend to relinquish the original vowel sound (permitting the vowel focus to be weakened) when that vowel occurs on more than one note or on a melisma. This is especially true when the vocal tessitura lies across the passaggio. At this point the singer's mind is distracted from concentrating on the vowel sound because of the insecurity which he experiences in this area of his voice, and "migration" away from the core of the vowel then occurs. Again, I feel it is important to emphasize the point to which I referred in Chapter I, that the singer (and teacher) should not confuse cause and effect. Traditionally, voice teachers have instructed students to purposely think of migrating the vowel to some neutral sound such as "uh" for "AH" (called "covering") in order to make the transition into the upper range. However, my view is that this practice usually produces a dull, labored tone. Most certainly, the vowel quality undergoes a change as the singer ascends upward in range, but that change is effect, not cause. If the singer envisages the correct vowel sound (cause) and adds the proper amount of space as the note(s) in a particular range dictate(s), the effect will be that the vowel has migrated. For example, "EE" sounds more like "ih" on g^2 and higher pitches in the soprano voice, but the singer needs to keep the core sound of the "EE" sharply focused in her mind, so that the vocal production

can avoid being too heavy. Thus, instead of retreating further from the vowel focus into more diffusion of tone, the
singer should concentrate more sharply upon the vowel sound
he should be producing at this point. A clearer conception
of the vowel, therefore, will help the singer over the "break"
(passaggio) with greater skill and better tone quality as well
as giving him more consistently even vocal production. The
clearly-produced vowel, combined with the release of jaw
tension, will permit a natural, lighter adjustment of the vocal
musculature for singing in the upper range.

The tenor recitative "Comfort Ye, My People," from
Handel's Messiah serves as an apt illustration of how singers
tend to migrate from the focal point of the vowel. Many
tenors will fail to form correctly the modified (open Italian)
"oh" sound in "comfort." (See Vowel Spectrum for modified
"oh".) The most common error in pronunciation is to migrate toward "aah" or "uh," producing "comfaahrt" or "com-
fuhrt." This pronunciation usually invites vocal tension and
engages the "chest" voice position of the vocal musculature.
This, in turn, produces a heavy or sometimes harsh sound
frequently incapable of ascending to the proper pitch.

To avoid this spreading and diffusing of the vowel,
the tenor singer should form an open Italian "oh" sound
(with forward focus) as he crosses the f♯ and g♯ of "fort"
allowing a natural adjustment to the head voice as illustrated
below, in a passage from the Messiah:

Figure 27, Use of Modified "oh" (Open Italian oh) Vowel.

Shaping the oral pharynx precisely "around" the modified "oh" helps to focus the tone and to keep the tone (vowel) from spreading. Precise focus upon a vowel also encourages the natural use of the "head voice"; lack of vowel focus causes breathy tones or dark sounds. Sharply focused vowels will produce clear tones, which are needed for resonance in the higher part of the male head register.

It is important to stress again that tone diffusion is caused by lack of vowel definition, which is especially noticeable across the passaggio (about e to f♯ in the tenor voice.) A further observation centers upon the problem of vowel diffusion on lower notes. Since we are using the tenor voice as an example, let us continue with an illustration from the aria "Every Valley Shall Be Exalted" from the same oratorio. Many tenors tend to ignore the core of the vowel sound "aw" in the word "exalted." This aria has many notes on one vowel sound (melisma). Consequently, the vowel tends to "disintegrate" into a diffused "uh" sound as the singer traverses these long phrases on that single vowel. If the vowel is permitted to become diffused, the resultant tone also becomes unfocused and weak, especially in the lower notes. By maintaining a firm "aw" vowel (not letting it become "uh") and being certain to focus the tone in the mask, the tenor will produce a stronger, more even tone color throughout the passage. This practice will aid also in developing flexibility to "negotiate" the rapid pace required to sing passages, such as these.

The application of the concept shown in Fig. 28 of maintaining vowel focus throughout a melisma in choral singing is illustrated in Fig. 29, this time using a modified "oh" vowel.

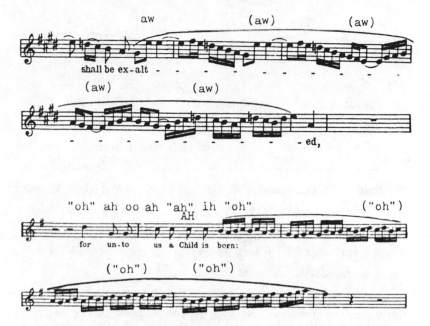

Top: Figure 28, Maintenance of Vowel Form "aw" on a Melisma. Bottom: Figure 29, Maintenance of Vowel Form "oh" on a Melisma. Both passages are from Handel's "Messiah."

The singers should be encouraged to write "oh" in their scores at the beginning of each measure of a long run of notes. This will remind them that they are to maintain a focused sound throughout the phrase, which will result in firmer tone quality and better flexibility and blend in the choir.

It is important to emphasize that clear vowel production will eliminate the necessity of over-emphasizing diphthongs and consonants. This is not to say that diphthongs and consonants are to be neglected; and certainly, they should be pronounced clearly. (The concept of consonants being

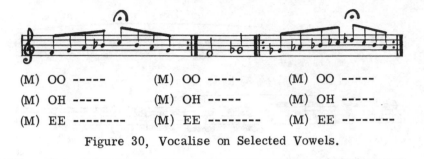

(M) OO -----   (M) OO -----   (M) OO -----

(M) OH -----   (M) OH -----   (M) OH -----

(M) EE --------   (M) EE --------   (M) EE --------

Figure 30, Vocalise on Selected Vowels.

"in line" with the vowel will be developed in detail in Chapter V.) Keeping this concept in mind, the choir director should stress the accurate pronunciation of the basic vowel sounds. The central idea is to keep the mind sharply focused upon the specific vowel sound at all times.

An especially good vocalise for training the mind of the singer to preserve the proper vowel focus is the sequence of OO - OH - EE vowels in a series of five notes up and down the scale, sung at mezzopiano to mezzoforte volume (see Fig. 30). It is beneficial, in identifying proper vowel (tone) production, for the singer to pause on the highest note of this five-tone vocalise to ascertain ("listen" and "feel") whether there is proper vowel focus. Also, the tempo of the exercise should be adjusted to the singer's ability. An "M" may be added up front, making the sound MOO (MOH and MEE).

The most important factor to remember is to maintain the focus of the vowel as the singer "negotiates" the five-note scale in a very legato style. No staccato singing should be applied here, because this tends to constrict the vocal apparatus. The tones should "flow" up and down.

VOWEL SPECTRUM

The Neglected Short "ah" Sound

An important consideration is the pronunciation of
"ah" (the shortest version of "AH") as it appears in speech
in "the, us, " or "but" as applied in the Vowel Spectrum
under "modified vowels. " This again, is one of the sounds
which tends to be neglected through faulty speech habits, the
most common being that the vowel duration is too short to
be "deeply set " for singing. In speaking, only the suggestion
of the "ah" is required to establish the intended sound. In
singing, however, the duration of the vowel sound depends
upon the time value of the note, sometimes requiring the
singer to sustain the tone (and thus the vowel sound) for
several beats. The short "ah" sound, then, is unpleasant
when the vocalist tries to sing it as he would speak it, because it has such dull acoustical characteristics.

The singer's attention should be drawn to the fact that
in singing, the short (neutral) forms of "ah" (such as "the, "
"a, " "cut, " etc.) must be deepened or slightly lengthened
enough in duration to resemble ah, as in "mother. " The
so-called "schwa" is the unstressed form of the short "ah"
as in "sofa" and "idea. " Both of these vowel forms are
almost identical when translated into sustained tone production. The two IPA symbols [ʌ] and [ə] are replaced here
in singing by the simple "ah" designation, which suffices to
form the proper mouth shape for singing this vowel in either
form, stressed or schwa. Of course, one must caution that
the pronunciation of "the" with the same depth of tone as
"father" (AH) would be ludicrous.

91

Left: Figure 31, Misuse of "uh" Vowel; right: Figure 32, Recommended Use of Various Vowel Forms.

There is no such thing as a short vowel in singing: that is to say the snappy, tight sound that usually comes when we speak such words as 'cot, eat, cut.' Singing does away with these almost entirely. [14]

Another example concerning the use of the short vowel is the singing of "Gloria" from the 12th Mass, attributed to Mozart: "Glorious is Thy name" (etc.). If a choir sings the passage shown in Fig. 31 as in conversational, short sounds, the tone quality (and rhythm) of the eighth-note value suffers greatly. In the illustration of the Mozart "Gloria," the tone on "Thy" tends to be almost completely lost and the eighth-note tends to be shortened to a sixteenth-note duration. The pronunciation of "Thy" usually becomes "Thuh." If the singers will produce a deeper "ah" quality (as in "mother") instead of "uh," for "Glorious" and father "AH" for "Thy," both rhythm and tone quality will be improved. For the best focus of tone, it is suggested that the choir think of the vowel sounds shown in Fig. 32. In concentrating upon the clearly-produced "father AH" for "Thy," the singers will inflect, quite naturally, the vanishing "ee" at the last split second. It should be noted also that the "oh" in "glorious" is conceived as being the open Italian "oh," the "r" requiring that it remain open instead of the closed "OH" in "go." This qualification will be discussed in detail later in this chapter under the heading of "modified" vowels.

Figure 33, Recommended Use of "uh" (Schwa) Vowel.

The Use of the "uh" Vowel Sound

The "uh" is used here as a replacement of the International Phonetic Alphabet neutral [ʌ] or schwa [ə] sound. The short, shallow "uh," as we speak it, is valuable in connecting words and also is effective in dramatic fortissimo endings of labials (M, B, P, F and V), linguals (L, N and R), dentals (T and D), sibilants (S, C, and Z) and palatines

93

(K, C and G). However, this short, unresonant sound cannot be sustained with any degree of pharyngeal depth. Nevertheless, it has a distinct place in vocal performance, namely, the retaining of firmness of sound produced by the principal vowel(s) contained in the respective words. The student should experiment by adding "uh" to each of the above-mentioned consonants with words such as "realm" (r-eh-l-m-u̲h̲), rob (r-AH-b-u̲h̲), etc., when singing forte. The important fact to remember here is that t̲h̲e̲ "u̲h̲" c̲l̲a̲r̲i̲f̲i̲e̲s̲ s̲i̲n̲g̲i̲n̲g̲ p̲r̲o̲n̲u̲n̲c̲i̲a̲t̲i̲o̲n̲ w̲h̲e̲n̲ a̲ f̲o̲r̲c̲e̲f̲u̲l̲ word-ending i̲s̲ n̲e̲e̲d̲e̲d̲. The "uh" must always be pronounced at lightning speed or else it will sound affected. There must be merely a s̲u̲g̲g̲e̲s̲-t̲i̲o̲n̲ o̲f̲ i̲t̲s̲ s̲o̲u̲n̲d̲, rather than an obvious pronunciation. An example of the "uh" used in this fashion is found in the text of the ancient Scottish folk song, "The Bonnie Earl O'Moray," which is sung forte in a sustained manner, especially when utilizing the Scottish brogue.

It must be stressed that the "uh" sound should not be overemphasized to the extent that it is out of character with the mood of the song. Native Italians are skilled in the use of "uh" for these purposes. This small vowel must be pronounced only as necessary to establish a link between two consonants, or to finish a word more dramatically, and it must be done with great care lest the singer sound artificial. In this respect it is evident that many consonants are associated with actual sounds and are sung to specific pitches. As one can see from the above example, the "uh" sound utilizes d(uh), s(zuh), n(uh), y(uh), trilled r(uh), t(uh), g(uh), in order to provide the firmness of tone and diction for these dramatic word endings.

VOWEL SPECTRUM

"Sub-Vowels"

In addition to the two categories of vowel sounds discussed so far (the principal vowel and the derivative vowel), there is a third category which I identify with singing: the liquid consonants. These are called "sub-vowels," because they possess distinctive, sonorous characteristics identified with pitch; that is, they can be sung on a "vocal line" just as any other vowel, except with less sonority and volume. (Some writers refer to these sounds as "semi-vowels" or "consovowels"; these two terms appear to be synonymous with "sub-vowels.") They are "sub-vowel" in their sound because they can, and should be given pitch recognition in singing. These sub-vowels are:

m, n, ng, l, r(uhr), v, z

They are listed here in order of their singability. The humming sound "m" is quite singable; a little less sonorous are the "n" and "ng." The sounds "m, n," and "ng" retain their "native" humming quality when used in the middle of a word, thus becoming a liaison between vowels. These "sub-vowels" must retain the humming sound especially in legato singing. Even the "v" and "z" are capable of pitch identification. They should maintain a maximum resonance in order to sustain the sound of legato singing.

"Amen" becomes "ahm" (as in humming)--"mehn." A reminder to the singer to "hum through" these sounds will help him to identify "m, n," and "ng" with specific pitches in words such as "come" and "sing."

An example of this is found in Gounod's "Oh, Divine Redeemer" and is shown in Fig. 34. Legato singing is analogous to a clothesline on which clothing is hung. The

95

Figure 34, Employment of "N" and "M" in Legato Singing.

---

line is continuous, the clothes being the vowels, while the clothes-pins are the consonants. The "clothesline" (tone) should appear to be continuous in legato singing. Therefore, the "m" and "n" sub-vowels should be produced with a great amount of intensity in order to sustain the tone for true legato singing.

The letter "l" begins with the sound of the vowel derivative "eh," but, as soon as the "l" is added, the tongue lifts up behind the front teeth, making the tone less singable. Nevertheless, the student should give particular attention to singing on these "sub-vowel" sounds, verifying that the lips and tongue are free of tension. A vowel derivative sound "uhr" [replacing the IPA (r)] (as in ever) likewise sustains the "r" in speech. If "r" is sung as one often hears it spoken in American English, a hard, raspy sound results. Many singers and vocalists eliminate the reference to the "r" by substituting a form of "ah." Then, the sound becomes "evah." This diction is out of character with normally spoken American English and should be pronounced as "uhr." (See Vowel Spectrum, p. 69.) When the singer understands the respective function of these "specialized" singing sounds and their relationship to pitch, he possesses a valuable insight into the singing process.

Modified Vowels

Another area which needs clarification is the recogni-

tion of the existence of modified vowels. Some vowel
sounds, when combined with other sounds, tend to lose their
initial identities and their purity--when we speak them. Yet,
in singing, we must give these vowel sounds a definite focal
point. These modified sounds are mainly "oh," "oo" and
"ah" as defined in the Vowel Spectrum. The "oh" in "forth"
or "glorious" are prime examples. Some persons advise
pronunciation of the word "forth" as "fawrth," but this pronunciation produces a broad and diffused (unfocused) tone
and also muddies diction. The singer is able to focus the
sound much more accurately if he thinks of the open Italian
"oh" sound as the focal point, and then proceeds (as he
sings it) to pronounce the word: "foh-rth." (See an example of this in Fig. 27 [page 87], the tenor recitative
"Comfort Ye, My People.") This is also true when the
"oh" sound is combined with the vanishing "ee." The singer
should pronounce the word "voice" as "voh-eece" (vanishing
"ee") rather than as a mixture, "vaw-ce." The vowel "oh"
in this example is again the open Italian "oh."

Another sound, which is often mispronounced in singing is the "OO" in "surely." When sung "shOO-rly," instead
of "sh-uuh-rly," the tone produced is a more focused sound.

Treatment of Diphthongs

The combination of two vowel sounds is termed a
diphthong. In spoken English, one combines the two sounds
as though they were one. The requirements of sustained
sounds in singing, however, demand that one of the two
sounds be more prominent in order to maintain the focal
point of the tone. Failure to focus upon one of the two vowel

sounds results in an indefinite, often shallow sound. "Muddy" vowels are the root of most of the diction problems of singers. A clearly produced vowel is quite naturally contrasted with other vowel sounds and consonants. Thus, when accurately produced, the clearly-defined vowel usually eliminates the need for radical stress of consonants. Over-emphasis on hard consonants tends to destroy the vocal line, for the consonant must always lead smoothly into the vowel which follows it. Ordinarily, it is the first of the two sounds which should be given the longer duration, except the English "u," which becomes "ee-OO." The second part of the diphthong should be considered as a consonant or as part of a consonant whenever there is one to which it may be attached. The words "trout" or "thou" provide an example. They are a mixture of the two vowels "AH" and "oo." Note that if the two vowel sounds are "mixed," the result is a sound similar to "aw." If one sings "trout" as "trawt," the tone usually becomes diffused and flacid, having no particular definition. This is another example of how lack of precise vowel definition weakens tone quality and muddies diction. For this reason, it is difficult to understand the words which many choirs, and individuals, sing. The singer, therefore, must pronounce the word "trout" as "trAH--oot," the second (vanishing) part of the diphthong being attached directly to the consonant "t." The sound of longest duration and of most prominence is "AH." In the case of "thou," the pronunciation is "thAH" with "oo" acting in the role of finishing the word.

An especially mispronounced diphthong is found in words such as "might," "sight," "like," etc. Realistically, this vowel is the "father AH" plus the vanishing "ee," the latter sound combining with the consonant to conclude the word. Frequently, one hears the vowel "I" sung as "uh" or "oy" when the singer "migrates" from the core of the "AH" sound toward the vanishing "ee." Then, the only recourse the singer has is instinctively to darken the "ee" sound. The "uh" or "oy" sound is completely out of character with clear diction. One cannot sing the English diphthong "I." It must be "AH" + "ee" as the Italian language dictates.

Reinforcement of this concept can be found in the manner in which the Italians treat multiple vowels. The stronger of two vowel sounds is always given longer duration, even though the weak vowel is also clearly defined, though of shorter duration. When the weaker of the two sounds is adjacent to a consonant, the weaker vowel and the consonant are combined. This results not only in a stronger focus and identification of the sound, but it also provides for clear diction and intensified sustaining of the sound throughout the duration of the note value. For all practical purposes in singing, diphthongs are really compound vowels consisting of one weak and one strong sound. The following examples, sung on any given pitch, should be considered. The diphthong in

> "so" is pronounced OH + oo, the vanishing "oo" acting in the capacity of a consonant to finish the word.
>
> "say" is pronounced AY + ee, the vanishing "ee" acting in the capacity of a consonant, and pronounced at the final duration of the note value.
>
> "ice" is pronounced AH + eece.
>
> "house" is pronounced AH + oose.
>
> "boy" is pronounced oh + ee (open Italian "oh").

"new" is pronounced ee + OO (in this example, the
first sound is the weaker one and the sustaining
sound is on the second one, i.e., "OO.")

"we" is pronounced oo + EE.

The same principle applies to triphthongs, exemplified by
"pure" (ee + OO + uhr). One must be aware, however,
that these weak beginning and ending vowel sounds are very
short in duration; nevertheless, they should be precisely
focused.

Singing in the Extremes of the Vocal Range

The singer should be reminded that he must maintain
the high and narrow arch of the oral pharynx and that he
must clearly define the vowel (which is synonymous with
tonal focus), in order to sing high notes effectively. (The
use of the Vowel Spectrum can be especially helpful in teaching singers to use their voices in sustained high tessitura.)
The high and narrow arch of the oral pharynx and the clearly
defined vowel, when combined with the method of breathing
to be described in Chapter VI, greatly assist singers to extend their ranges in both directions. It is also important
to remind the singers that the sensation they should experience in the oral cavity is similar to that felt at the beginning
of a yawn. (Note the feeling of flared nostrils.) This sensation, coupled with clear vowel pronunciation and focus behind the upper front teeth, greatly assist the singer in maintaining the correct "voice placement" as the scale is ascended.

Again, the problem of "cover" may raise a question
in the reader's mind, particularly in the male voice. My
definition of the term "cover" is the avoidance of "wide-open"

tones across the passaggio. I use the term advisedly and
carefully with students, so as not to confuse cause and effect.
I prefer not to conceive of darkening the tone, or the concept of vowel migration, across the passaggio. Rather, the
effect of less-open tones over the passaggio can be caused
by adding the correct amount of space (arching the soft palate) to clearly-defined vowels. The singer must form the
vowel accurately, but he should also employ a "snarl" or
"sneer" in order to "project" the tone "forward." Vowel
depth provides the necessary "cover," while accurate formation of the vowel prevents excessive over-formation or "darkness" of vowel and tone color. It is important for the singer to lower or relax the arch of the soft palate ever so
slightly as he approaches the passaggio to attain a more
forward vowel (tone) projection. I term this the "forward
thrust" of the projected vowel. This lowering or relaxing
of the soft palate prevents the focus of the tone from dropping back into the throat. Be especially careful not to over-
form the vowel over the passaggio lest the tone become dull
and dark. The passaggio will be discussed more fully in
Chapter IV.

All voices capable of producing the falsetto should
practice this, especially tenors. The use of the falsetto to
produce high notes, when combined with slight arching of the
soft palate and effective breath management, provides the
basis of sotto voce (soft voice) singing in the upper range.
Furthermore, the falsetto helps to keep the singer from producing a strained quality when he cannot reach high notes
with "full voice" and its use develops strength in the muscles
which are employed in singing above the passaggio. (Many
male singers fail to develop the falsetto because it sounds

101

so weak in the early stages of vocal development. When the falsetto position of the vocal folds is combined with the "forward thrust"--and not an over-formed vowel--it gives more "bite" and fundamental to the tone.) It is the sharp focus of the vowel which adds strength to the lighter head tones such as the falsetto. This is achieved through employment of the "snarl or sneer" feeling as mentioned earlier. More discussion of the falsetto will be presented in Chapter IV.

In producing extremely low notes, the singer must continue to concentrate upon very accurate vowel formation. This concept is based upon the principle that the clearly defined vowel has more sonority than the weak, diffused vowel, especially on high and low notes. Clearly defining the vowel in the lower part of the range helps to keep the pharyngeal area focused more firmly, but there must be less arching of the soft palate for the lower pitches. Many skilled singers (especially lyric and coloratura sopranos) tend to keep the soft palate raised too high as they descend to the lower extremes of their vocal ranges (from f above middle c on down). Clear pronunciation of the vowel shapes the contour of the oral pharynx properly for the particular pitch and vowel being sung, while the singer maintains the arch of this soft palate strictly in relation to the height of the pitch; i.e., the arch should rise gradually as the pitch rises. (As has been mentioned previously, the arching adjustment of the soft palate is very small from pitch to pitch, so the singer must not "over-yawn" as the scale gradually ascends by half or whole steps.)

In summary, the singer must always confine the tone within the "vessel" (vowel).

Resonance in Singing

The various concepts of the term "resonance" cause controversy among choral conductors and vocal teachers. Some authorities maintain that singing resonance cannot be developed by humming musical selections and exercises.[15] Others are convinced that humming suggests a "forward placement" or sensation of the tone which, in turn, promotes the fundamental vocal tone.[16] If humming is correctly produced with a completely released jaw,* it serves as a bridge from the "chest" voice to the "head" voice, or _falsetto_, because, in humming, the singer tends to use the vocal mechanism more lightly than he does in singing on vowel sounds. (This is especially true for the upper regions of the voice.) Humming aids the singer in experiencing phonation with the light approximation (touching) of the vocal bands in the upper register of the voice. It is virtually impossible to hum in "chest voice" above the male (or contralto) "break," unless the jaw is free of tension, i.e., "released." (Also see description of this term in Glossary, page 195.)

According to Webster, resonance is the "intensification and enrichment of a musical tone by means of supplementary vibration." Vocalists and teachers frequently use the term "resonance" synonymously with the term "tone quality." A voice rich in "color" is often referred to as a "resonant voice."

> ... [T]he chief element in determining tone quality of the human voice is the shape of the resonating air cavities above the vocal cords.[18]

---

*I prefer to avoid the term "relaxed," because it implies weakness. On the other hand, "released" means to be set free from restraint, to be liberated (from inordinate tension).

Thus, the mouth and throat mechanically amplify sounds, much as the old pre-electric era gramophone horns amplified the vibrations produced by the needle in the record groove. It is axiomatic, then, that the singer must seek to capitalize upon the maximum amount of amplification of sound in relation to volume needed; thus, the importance of tonal focus through efficient vowel formation.

Resonance and Tone Quality
(Also see "The Resonators" in Chapter II)

In order to determine the relationship between resonance and tone quality in singing, we can look again to the vowel. Good tone quality and resonance depend upon satisfactory vowel production, because it is the latter which gives character to sound. Nature has endowed some individuals with better physical resources than others, i. e., mouth "architecture," plasticity and strength of the vocal musculature. Even though the shape of the resonator and the coordination of the muscles influence tone quality and vocal resonance, everyone, despite physical limitations, can improve vocal resonance through a "properly shaped" vowel for each given pitch and word.

The analogy of the human voice to a wind instrument has been commonly accepted for years. This is confirmed by Redfield's theory:

> The quality of tone produced by such an instrument (mouthpiece plus cylindrical pipe or cavity) is always dependent upon two main factors: the manner in which the generator vibrates and the shape of the resonator.[18] [See Fig. 14, page 50.]

To elaborate: (1) The vocal folds vibrate in the

larynx, thus disturbing the molecules of air. This is the
fundamental sound, similar to that which the mouthpiece of
a trumpet or clarinet produces and has little resonance itself.
The sound needs amplification.

(2) The ventricles (false vocal folds) are housed in
the laryngopharynx. They rise and almost close during
phonation, and thus create between them and the true vocal
folds another potential resonating system, referred to as the
"ventricles of the larynx."[19]

(3) Then, the oral pharynx serves to further amplify
and give character (tone and vowel color) to the fundamental
sound produced. This is called the timbre of a voice and is
similar to the effect which the tubing of a trumpet or other
wind instrument has upon the amplification of sounds produced
by the mouthpieces.

(4) The tongue, interacting with the soft and hard
palates and the teeth, allows articulation of words for communication. This area between the tongue and palates allows
for flexibility of sound and nuance of tone color. The tongue
should always be free of tension and be as low in the mouth
as each vowel formation will permit. This provides optimum
space for amplification of the sound produced by the vocal
bands.

(5) The lips "round off" (provide the finishing form
for) the character of the sound.

Consideration of the vocal process with these basic
terms gives the singer a clear, simple picture of the components of his "instrument." This, in turn, enables him to
understand the relationship of the vowel to vocal production.
It bears repeating that the singer should recognize that every
pitch in vocal music has an individual shape and size.

Therefore, he can appreciate the need for proper coordination of the mouth cavity and the tongue. He should not think of their functions separately, but rather as the product of correct vowel pronunciation related to depth of tone.

Again, it is important to stress that the slight yawning feeling is the means by which the singer provides the necessary space to make the spoken vowel resonant and amplified in the singing process. The "snarl" or "sneer" projects the tone (vowel) farther forward behind the upper front teeth, and prevents the tone from becoming wide and spread as does the "smile," which is often employed in order to project the tone forward.

To recapitulate, the main emphasis should be on the proper shaping of the resonator through proper pronunciation of the vowel and consonant. This is a tangible means by which the unskilled singer can learn basic techniques of singing and the skilled singer can improve his vocal production.

Tone Placement

This term is one which is often misused in vocal work. It can be clarified, however, in a few concise sentences: the tone cannot be successfully aimed or placed by some mechanical manner such as an instrumentalist would do in terms of embrochure or piano hand technique. Rather, a well-focused, resonant sound is the result of coordinating all the factors of singing with the singular effort of producing sound; the <u>fundamental</u> <u>element</u> <u>of</u> <u>focusing</u> <u>this</u> <u>sound</u> <u>production</u> <u>is</u> <u>proper</u> <u>vowel</u> <u>formation</u>. The intensity of the stream of water through a nozzle is dependent upon the size of the orifice through which the water flows. It can be adjusted

106

to accommodate various sizes of the stream of water while the pressure remains the same. In such a way, vowels have their peculiar sizes and shapes, but the volume of energy remains constant. Thus, the volume of water or sound which emanates from the mouth of the hose or the singer's oral cavity remains comparable; the nozzle or the vowel shape governing the concentration of water or vocal energy. Specifically, the volume of sound passing through the oral cavities is governed finally by the shape and size of the resonators. Thus, the proper adjustment of the resonators results in a more focused (placed) tone. It is the intensity (focus) of tone which produces the effect of loud volume--in other words "impacted tone" which has a deep and yet "narrow channel" guiding it to a focal point behind the upper front teeth.

It is a curious phenomenon that the more brilliant sounds in the high register actually are richer and fuller than the dull, heavy and thick production, because the "highs" give a more comprehensive scope to the tones of the upper part of the voice. Most tyro singers produce a basically focused tone; it is just incomplete--lacking "depth" and thus the lower partials of the pitch.

In Summary

The Vowel Spectrum is a simplified system of phonetics which adapts itself to natural, instinctive singing. It avoids the complicated IPA, which is more effective in language study. The singer should not be inhibited by unnecessary details. He must be free to express himself artistically. Therefore, the more simplified the concept of vocal production can be, the more readily the vocalist can attain this objective. This approach to singing is based strictly upon the application of the vowel to the process of singing.

The vowel must always be focused high in the arch of the hard palate (behind the front teeth). If the focal point drops down in the floor of the mouth, the tone becomes dull and heavy, also prohibiting proper transition to the upper voice.

To achieve this "forward focus," the singer should utilize the "snarl" or "sneer" coupled, of course, with the employment of the slight yawn to combine the "velvet" (soft palate lower partials) with the "brass" (hard palate high partials). Again, it is important to stress that the jaw must not be jammed open, but rather to "float" as if suspended by rubber bands.

One helpful concept is to think space behind the clearly (forward) produced vowel, which has its feel of focus on the upper front teeth.

A former student of mine once stated in the vernacular, "Your method gets the 'mostest' from the 'leastest' in the 'shortest' possible time, because it is so logical and uncomplicated." This may be an overstatement, but I have found that the correct utilization of the Vowel Spectrum can be a thoroughly useful tool in improving the singing technique of the student in the choral ensemble as well as the vocal studio.

References

[1]E. Herbert-Caesari, The Voice of the Mind (London: Robert

Hale, 1951), p. 88.

[2]Charles K. Scott, The Fundamentals of Singing (New York: Pitman Pub. Corp., 1954), p. 218.

[3]Harry R. Wilson, Artistic Choral Singing (New York: G. Schirmer, 1959), p. 162.

[4]Mario P. Marafioti, Caruso's Method of Voice Production (1922) (reprinted, Austin, Texas: Cadica Enterprises, 1958), p. 69.

[5]Ibid., p. 65.

[6]Lilli Lehman, How to Sing (New York: Macmillan, 1929), p. 215.

[7]Douglas Stanley, Your Voice: Applied Science of Vocal Art (New York: Pitman Pub. Corp., 1945), p. 69.

[8]Richard Luchsinger and Godfrey Arnold, Voice-Speech-Language (Belmont, Calif.: Wadsworth Pub. Co., 1965), p. 32.

[9]Johan Sundberg, "The Acoustics of the Singing Voice," Scientific American 236:3 (March 1977), 86.

[10]Ralph D. Appelman, The Science of Vocal Pedagogy (Bloomington: Indiana University Press, 1967), p. 173.

[11]Wilson, Artistic Choral Singing, p. 161.

[12]Ibid., p. 164.

[13]Appelman, The Science, pp. 299-303.

[14]Scott, The Fundamentals, p. 405.

[15]Wilson, Artistic, p. 185.

[16]John Carroll Burgin, Teaching Singing (Metuchen, N.J.: Scarecrow Press, Inc., 1973), p. 94. Also Victor Fields, Training the Singing Voice (New York: Kings Crown Press, 1947), p. 144.

[17]John Redfield, Music: A Science and an Art (New York: Tudor Pub. Co., 1928), p. 268.

[18]Ibid., p. 267.

[19]Appelman, The Science, p. 77.

Chapter IV

THE PASSAGGIO AND FALSETTO

THE PASSAGGIO

The passaggio is the passageway from the lower voice to the upper voice. It involves two or three musical intervals in which the voice either breaks or where there is uncertainty of vocal production. Mature singers usually have "ironed out" this break over the passaggio by "thinning out" the mass of the vocal folds as they approach what would be the actual breaking point.

Singing above the "break" in the falsetto position naturally produces weak sounds in early vocal training, because of the underdeveloped nature of the muscles governing phonation in the upper vocal range. The tyro singer should note that the falsetto voice becomes stronger as he progresses farther above the "break" until he reaches the end of this "register," with its zipper-like action. All too many young singers avoid singing falsetto because it sounds so breathy and weak, thus erroneously believing that it is incorrect vocal production. I have found the falsetto to be the undeveloped and "unplaced" head voice: voce di testa [head] (alias falsetto) versus voce di petto [chest voice].

The solution to the problem of the passaggio is difficult to put into words. Some singers have more trouble with this area of the voice than others. Also, some teachers

refuse to recognize it, stating that there is no such phenomenon as a "break" or that "registers" do not exist.   Ideally,
there should be no vocal break.   However, when a "break"
occurs in any voice, it is a clear indication that there is a
muscle imbalance over the span of two or three notes in
which the problem occurs.   It is, therefore, imperative that
both teacher and student work intelligently toward its solution.

Weldon Whitlock is one of the few authors I have encountered who discusses the problem in depth.   I shall refer below to the points he makes in his article for the NATS
Bulletin and his books, Bel Canto for the Twentieth Century
and Facets of the Singer's Art.

First, Whitlock admonishes the reader that the passaggio problem will not disappear by itself.   "It must be
slowly and painstakingly worked out."[1]

> The tones just before the break, the pre-passaggio
> tones, are of the greatest possible importance.   If
> these tones have been balanced, there is no accu-
> mulation of tension, and when the jaw is dropped,
> usually the voice will turn quite freely.[2]

Whitlock uses the term "turning" to describe going smoothly
from one register to another.

> The point of the tone in the 'heady' upper register
> must come in first when any correct tone is re-
> leased.   The singer moves from one tone to an-
> other on this point.[3]

The problem centers around the fact that singers do
not lighten the tone in the pre-passaggio tones just below the
break.   E. Herbert-Caesari refers to this as failing to
"eliminate the mass."

112

> In short, 'elimination' means that as the pitch
> rises, so the vibrator 'grows small by degrees,
> and beautifully less'; it means a gradual shedding
> of the load. [4]

This action is accomplished by mentally envisioning a lighter
texture as the singer approaches the passaggio, thus properly engaging the cricoarytenoid and cricothyroid muscles in
the process. Again, this theory supports by concept of the
proper aural image the singer must have for the mind to
direct the musculature to function properly. When the jaw
is free from tension and the vowel is pure, the adjustment
or "turning," as Whitlock terms it, will begin to take place.
"Keep in mind that tension is the archfoe of the equalization
of the registers. "[5]

Probably the most universal approach to the concept
of developing a lighter texture in the passaggio is to utilize
the falsetto or "head voice" from the top down. (Discussion
of the falsetto comes later in this chapter.)

Since the passaggio problem occurs more obviously in
men's voices than in women's, we might well begin our discussion of the solution to the problem by citing examples
pertaining to the male voice.

The "break" in the tenor voice is usually between e
natural and g above middle c, and in the baritone between
d and e natural (occasionally as high as f above middle c).

The tenor should begin a descent of falsetto or "head
voice" tones on the vowel "OO" or "m" (humming freely) on
a above middle c at mezzopiano volume and carry the notes
downward five notes (later employing an entire octave when
more facility is gained). Then, slowly work the vocalization
down by half steps so that the top note of the exercise

is middle c. The vowel "EE" should be employed in this vocalise also.

When the student has developed some insight into the lighter tone quality necessary for singing across the passaggio, octave skips using a glissando or portamento up and down, or down and up, may be employed, beginning on about c below middle c for the tenor. It is well to pause on the top note until tonal focus is ascertained before the downward glissando. This exercise assists the singer in achieving a lighter approximation of the vocal folds across the problem area from below. (See Fig. 23, page 76.)

> Constantly watch that the jaw stays down and loose.
> Raise this scale gradually by half steps, until the
> starting one is B natural for the tenor.[6]

The entire exercise should be sung molto legato. The utilization of the supported tone glissando keeps the vocal folds phonating, for I have observed that if the singer sings only the bottom and top notes, the vocal folds become too heavily approximated on top. The glissando helps to thin out the mechanism as the voice crosses the passaggio.

Another vocalise for passaggio work is the OO - OH - EE or MM - OH - EE of Fig. 30 (see page 90). Repeat each sequence three times per vowel rather than changing vowels on each run. Begin in any comfortable range of the singer and ascend the beginning note by half steps over the passaggio at a suitable tempo. Other vowels can be introduced as the student develops facility. The volume should be no louder than mezzopiano to mezzoforte. The "EE" vowel especially helps to thin the vocal lips and encourages the action of "thinning out the mass."

The object of these vocalises, or any others dealing

114

with the passaggio problem, is to "eliminate the mass" (thickness) of the vocal fold approximation, so that there is a "bridge" between the lower and upper voices.

Again, I refer to the value of the correct image of the tone to be produced through clear voweling. I have found that a common contemporary idiom assists some of my students in developing an aural image of the tones they should "hear" (or "feel") across this problem area. I tell them to "think in stereo"; that is, envision both the lower and upper voice quality simultaneously so that the lighter quality is present, but the lower "body" quality is also evident. This assignment requires that the student be imaginative in his approach to singing. Also, I ask the student to meditate quietly in seclusion about imagining the two "registers" blending together to become one sound. This approach has been successful for me in a large number of cases, and is always effective with students who possess disciplined and imaginative minds.

> So, we can see that the problem of the Passaggio is one of developing each register so that both are of equal intensity. Intensity, is the musculature resistance against the breath pressure. This is the 'Crux' of the register difficulty. The intensity gives the tone the 'ping,' or 'bite.'[7]

The chart presented in Fig. 35 illustrates where and when the ideal muscle balance is acquired. The voice really has but these two extremes of color--the artist can balance them on an ascending or descending scale IF he has practiced messa di voce on almost every note in his scale. Messa di voce being an ornament of bel canto days fell by the wayside when we accepted the meatier style of singing. That was unfortunate since the practice of messa di voce

115

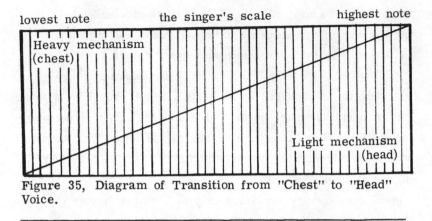

Figure 35, Diagram of Transition from "Chest" to "Head" Voice.

after the even scale has been attained cements its gains. Consider the "heady," "bright" element in the voice as the skeleton or bones upon which we hang the meaty side. The Fig. 35 chart is not completely accurate since the highest soprano's top notes will have none of the "chest" as will the lowest notes of the bass have none of the "head." However, it illustrates the need for balancing the heavy and light vocal mechanisms.

The opera singer is tempted to keep adding weight to the top, because it "brings down the galleries." When Bu-prez sang his high C in chest, it unseated the reigning tenor Nourrit at the Paris Opera. Caruso also fell victim to the extent that he had two operations for nodes during his career. It should be noted that when he died at age 49, his high C's were causing him trouble.

In my teaching experience I have found it most helpful to ask the student to "snarl" or "sneer" slightly (not smile) as he goes into the passaggio and upper range of the voice, using the falsetto concept of tone. This action gives intensity to the tone by also adding brilliance and body to the lighter quality required in that area of the voice.

Again, it is important for the student and teacher to realize that much patience and long-suffering is required to gain the necessary facility to negotiate the passaggio so that the "break" is eliminated.

THE FALSETTO

There is probably no other term in vocal parlance that causes more controversy than the word falsetto. It has been called "false resonance" as well as "pure tone." Vennard describes the action of the vocal musculature in his discussion of falsetto:

> In the light voice the thyro-arytenoids are not en-
> tirely passive, but comparatively so. ... With the
> vocalis muscle relaxed, it is possible for the crico-
> thyroids to place great longitudinal tension upon
> the vocal ligaments. The tension can be increased
> in order to raise the pitch even after the maximum
> length of the cords has been reached. This makes
> the folds thin so that there is negligible vertical
> phase difference, no such thing as the glottis open-
> ing at the bottom first and then at the top. The
> vocalis muscles fall to the sides of the larynx and
> the vibration takes place almost entirely in the liga-
> ments along the edges of the cords.... Such a vi-
> bration can take place at high frequencies, because
> there is very little mass to be moved, and the
> amplitude is small.... The folds offer much less
> resistance to the breath....[8]

The last sentence explains why the falsetto "register" is so weak and, often, breathy, i. e., there is very little resistance to the breath pressure exerted by the singer. We refer then to Whitlock, who maintains that the sets of mus- cles involved must be developed so that they are of equal intensity (strength).

In the lower tones of the falsetto (below and during the passaggio notes), the entire edges of the vocal folds vibrate. This produces a rather weak, breathy tone, but as the pitch rises, a damping action takes place (the zipper action to which I refer in Chapter II) so that much greater intensity of tone is produced.

It is my observation, based upon experience in the teaching studio, that when the vocal musculature becomes strongly enough developed in this area of the voice through some of the passaggio exercises described above, the so-called falsetto begins to assume some of the characteristics of the "head voice," which is regarded by most voice teachers as the preferable vocal quality which should be present in the upper range of any singer. The "head voice" is commonly understood to have more body of tone than that of the falsetto.

Husler and Rodd-Marling present an interesting view of the term falsetto. They state that, because there are two very opposing views of falsetto (one: a harmful, false voice; the other: a valuable attribute for the singing voice), it is obvious that two utterly different types of falsetto are involved:

> An extremely thin, breathy tone quality which cannot be modified; and which cannot become a transition to the full voice. They term it a "collapsed organ."

> A tone quality possessing greater tension, strength and carrying power; one which is modifiable to a certain extent and out of which the full voice can be developed--i.e., a supported falsetto. [9]

The authors conclude that there is another quality of register called the "head register" or "head tone." "This is a very light soaring sound, voluminous, but with no

118

particular tension or substance and no kernel."

> If the action of the muscle crico-pharyngeus (that
> draws the ring cartilage backwards and anchors it
> below to the gullet) is added to the process, the
> vocal folds are even more powerfully stretched.
> This produces what singers call the 'full tone of
> the head voice'.... 10

Husler and Rodd-Marling conclude that:

> Falsetto and head register are variants, therefore,
> of one and the same basic element; both qualities
> are brought about by the functions that stretch the
> vocal folds with little or no participation from the
> muscles imbedded in the folds themselves [thyro-
> arytenoids]. The difference between the two lies
> chiefly in the shaping of the glottal chink [vocal
> bands]; in falsetto it becomes shorter and narrower.

The question arises again: That is what should happen,
but how do I achieve this stronger head register tone, which
seems to be preferable?

My experience over many years of teaching is that
the "supported falsetto" is the first step toward the development of head voice. When the singer produces the "unsupported falsetto," I ask him to "snarl" or "sneer" so that the
"focal point" of the tone is in the mask--certainly as "nasty"
and (to him) as nasal as he can make it. I assure him that
he can always "yawn" a slight bit more to add warmth to the
tone, but that he must always project that falsetto voice very
far forward in order to give it some "ping" and intensity.

The above procedure has proven to be successful with
my own tenor voice as well as with my students. Eventually,
the somewhat weak falsetto develops strength and power, if
the student applies the principles of the more "forward
focus" of the tone--in the mask. Of course, this strength

and power assumes that the student is capable of adequate breath control also, so as to release the proper amount of breath required to activate the vocal folds in an efficient manner. (See Chapter VI.)

Again, we can refer to Whitlock's admonition that proper development of the passaggio (and in this case the "head voice" via the "supported" falsetto) requires a great amount of patience and time. Husler and Rodd-Marling conclude: "One thing is certain: a voice without a _falsetto_ is not a singing voice."[12]

The concept of "head resonance" is a helpful thought for developing the singer's upper range, i.e., the sensation of "head resonance," "tonal focus in the mask," and vibration in the "upper" resonance chambers.

> These sensations are the quality components that may be felt to predominate in the head, face, sinuses, nose and mouth, especially when the singer is using the upper range of his voice.... [13]

I am particularly committed in most cases to the use of the "supported falsetto" in the development of the young voices, with which I work. The student must make a conscientious effort to utilize the falsetto so that the true "head voice" can eventually emerge. There is no manner in which this process can be accelerated beyond the natural physical maturation of the particular singer, however.

A Note on the Word Falsetto

The _falsetto_ is rather a bad term which we have inherited from the early voice teachers, who were not concerned with scientific accuracy. Something not "natural" in vocal production was called "false." In the nineteenth century

120

PASSAGGIO AND FALSETTO

Garcia used three classifications, chest, falsetto and head, indicating that the falsetto was the middle "register." Even this great teacher contributed to the confusion of the terminology. However, no matter what terminology is used, the important factor we should consider is that the passaggio problem is best dealt with by working from the lighter top down over the "break."

References

[1] Weldon Whitlock, "The Problem of the Passaggio," NATS Bulletin 24:3 (February 1968), 10.

[2] Ibid.

[3] Ibid.

[4] E. Herbert Caesari, The Voice of the Mind (London: Robert Hale, 1951), p. 84.

[5] Weldon Whitlock, Bel Canto for the Twentieth Century (Milwaukee: Pro Musica Press, 1968), p. 68.

[6] Ibid., p. 69.

[7] Weldon Whitlock, Facets of the Singer's Art (Champaign, Ill.: Pro Musica Press, 1967), p. 33.

[8] William Vennard, Singing: The Mechanism and the Technic (New York: Carl Fischer, 1967), p. 67.

[9] Paraphrased from Frederick Husler and Yvonne Rodd-Marling, Singing: The Physical Nature of the Vocal Organ (New York: October House, 1965), p. 59.

[10] Ibid., p. 61.

[11] Ibid.

[12] Husler and Rodd-Marling, Singing, p. 61.

[13] Victor Fields, Foundations of the Singer's Art (New York: Vantage Press, 1977), p. 144.

Chapter V

CONSONANTS:
THEIR ROLE IN SINGING

There are at least three ways that consonants are treated in singing: they are ignored; they are over-emphasized to contrast with muddy voweling; and they are put to good use by keeping them in the track of, or "in line" with, the vowel which follows.

Definition of Consonants (in English)

> A speech sound produced by a partial or complete obstruction of the air stream by any of various constrictions of the speech organs [American Heritage Dictionary, 1973].

> A sound in speech, produced either by a complete momentary stoppage of the air stream in some part of the mouth cavity, or by the lips, as it passes from the lungs, or by a partial stoppage or constriction, sufficient to produce a distinct and perceptible friction. Those sounds accompanied by complete stoppage are called stops; those occurring during constriction of the mouth-passage are variously called open consonants, fricatives, spirants and continuants [Little & Ives Webster Dictionary, 1962].

The consonant, then, is regarded as a constriction of the breath channel, which interrupts the flow of sound emanating from the larynx. Some are voiced and are referred to in this study as sub-vowels: m, n, ng, l. r, v, z. Others

are voiceless and require an identification with a neutral
vowel sound, such as "eh," "uh," etc.

Wilson regards the use of the consonant in vocal
development as being limited,

> and in fact they can be actually detrimental....
> Consonants must not interfere with ... the basic
> resonance, breath action and vowel formations for
> singing. [1]

Fear of consonants causes many choral directors to
neglect them in order to retain the continuity of sound which
they desire. To this Wilson says, "No! Consonants must
be used to make diction understandable and expressive without distorting the singing tone." [2]

Advancing a step further, it will be noted that a consonant properly related to the vowel will help the singer to
express diction clearly without distorting the tone. The
"hard" consonants, such as b, d, g, j, k, p and t, tend to
constrict the throat as they are pronounced. The constriction
becomes more exaggerated as the pitch rises, unless the
singer allows for more oral space during the pronunciation
of the consonant, thus forming the buccalpharyngeal cavity
more like the vowel preceding or following it. This is the
source of my concept that the consonant must always be "in
line" with the vowel, so that a minimum of constriction takes
place in the buccalpharyngeal cavity during the articulation
of consonants. One can think the correct articulation of the
consonant (i.e., have an image) and still not impede vocal
production, if the "open throat" position is maintained similar
to that of the space needed for the neighboring vowels.

Fields comments on muscular movement in regard to
consonant articulation:

123

> If exaggerated, these movements of the speech or-
> gans may constrict and muffle the voice. There-
> fore, an economy-of-effort principle governs all
> articulatory action and it is necessary to learn to
> minimize transitional movements between sounds,
> especially during speedy utterance.[3]

There is great need, therefore, for the singer to relate the consonant to the vowel--to think of the vowel sound
he is about to produce while he is forming the consonant
which modifies it; to keep the soft palate arched while pronouncing consonants, particularly in the upper range of his
voice. This results in fewer major adjustments in the buccalpharyngeal cavity during the process of singing, thus assur-
ing smoother vocal production. Actually, if the soft palate
is consistently arched as needed for the respective height of
the pitches being produced, the movement from vowel to consonant to vowel will not "collapse" or constrict the soft palate during the pronunciation of the consonants. In other
words: keep the consonant "in line" with the vowel; i. e.,
the soft palate should be arched in a slightly yawning position
in consonant articulation. If the vowel is clearly produced,
there should be no reason to overemphasize the consonant,
putting it "out of line" with the vowel--and thus constricting
the throat and inhibiting vocal production in the process.
Even in staccato singing, where spaces are needed between
the sounds produced, the consonants should not constrict the
throat. The movement in the buccalpharyngeal cavity should
be handled carefully lest throat tension occur in the process.

There is further corroboration of the concept of arching the soft palate as one confronts the consonant in the act
of singing. In the German language the consonant "ch" for
the words "ich," "och" or "ach" are best pronounced by

retaining the vowel sounds through the consonant: EE(ch), "oh"(ch) and AH(ch). Keep the vowel formation in the oral pharynx as you breathe through the "ch" consonant; do not allow the soft palate to drop to a "k" position. (Some persons pronounce the German "ch" as "sh" [EE-sh, "oh"-sh and AH'sh], as do the South Germans and Viennese. Every singer is obligated to study language diction, not only for proper pronunciation of the language, but also because language facility leads directly to improved vocal production.) Be certain that the arch of the oral pharynx is kept high in the shape of those vowels so that the "ch" is almost inaudible. This tends to keep the throat open in the vowel position and the palate from collapsing. One of the greatest problems of the unskilled singer is mouth movements which vary significantly. These radical changes of the buccalpharyngeal cavity inhibit vocal production by constricting the throat. The objective, then, should be to prevent a wide variation in the oral pharynx between the vowel and the consonant.

If the principle stated above is generally applied to all English consonants (whether they appear before or after the vowel), there will be a minimal amount of adjustment for the buccalpharyngeal cavity to make in producing uniform tones. Consequently, the oral pharynx is not required to make radical changes from consonant to vowel to consonant, a process which tends to interrupt smooth vocal production. This is another reason why pure voweling is effective in singing: the consonant need not be emphasized to the point of distortion of sound if the vowel sound is clearly recognized. It should be emphasized also that "sluggish" consonants tend to cause "muddy" vowels.

The Consonant and the Singer's Range

On the lower notes of his range a singer can "afford"
to have more lip and mouth movement because the soft palate
is not raised as high as when the voice functions in the upper
part of the range and, consequently, there is less tension
throughout the vocal musculature. However, in the <u>upper</u>
<u>voice</u> <u>range</u> the singer must <u>treat</u> <u>the</u> <u>consonant</u> <u>less</u> <u>percus-</u>
<u>sively</u> than in the lower range, in order to keep the oral
cavity freely open for singing (something the native Italian
has always done). The intensity of the higher tessitura will
maintain the clarity of the consonants, even though the consonant articulation is lessened.

I have found that "Italianizing" consonants, such as
"t," "d," and "b" when singing English songs in higher tes-
situras, assists greatly in avoiding tension in the vocal tract.
This is to say that the consonant is, then, "in line" with the
vowel following it. By "Italianizing," I mean that more surface of the tongue touches the upper front teeth on "t's" and
"d's," and the lips are more relaxed for the articulation of
the "b's." It is as though the singer has a slight lisp in the
upper range.

Fields says, "The prime consideration in diction is
economy of movement in all working parts."[4] Excessive lip,
tongue and mouth movements in high-tessitura singing inhibit
vocal action. For instance, if a singer articulately pronounces on a high note, "t, g," or "d" as in "<u>that</u>," "Go<u>d</u>"
or "<u>done</u>," the oral pharynx will become significantly constricted. This is the result of the soft palate's dropping and
the tongue's rising to form the constriction (consonant). On
the other hand, if the singer carefully relates the consonant

to the deep-feeling sensation of the oral pharynx needed for high tone vowels, these conconants will become less percussive and thus the throat will not close when singing high tones. (Another way of stating this action is to "soften" the articulation of the consonant in the upper regions of the vocal range.) Moreover, as stated previously, the greater intensity of the higher tones negates the need of articulating the consonant in the same manner as the singer should do on lower pitches. These lower tones require a more "forward position" in order to provide a firm and clear timbre of sound.

Finally, the lips play an important role in the treatment of consonants. The lips should be free of tension, but they also should provide the final shaping of the consonant in order to clarify the diction of most words.

There is no mystery to the consonant in singing, providing it is always kept "in line" with the vowel.

References

[1] Harry R. Wilson, Artistic Choral Singing (New York: G. Schirmer, 1959), p. 185.

[2] Ibid., p. 123.

[3] Victor Fields, Foundations of the Singer's Art (New York: Vangard Press), 1977, p. 240.

[4] Ibid., p. 239.

Chapter VI

BREATHING AND POSTURE

Or: Stance and Respiration. The management of the
breath (often referred to as "breath control") must be developed by way of good posture, i. e., the alignment (stance)
of the body. "But," someone might ask, "What about opera
singers, who are often required to sing in awkward positions?" After years of well-established breath management,
a singer for whom a particular pose other than "concert
stance" is dictated, may be able to sing well in an ungainly
position. But first, one must achieve a well-balanced posture, in order that the "total instrument" of the singer can
function efficiently. The young singer, therefore, should
concentrate upon standing firmly erect--but comfortably--
with the pelvis "tucked in" as if sitting on the edge of a high
stool. When this posture is understood, the basic concept of
good breath management follows almost automatically. Good
posture leads up to the establishment of control over the abdominal muscles, which allows the singer to coordinate the
entire action as a unified feeling.

One may conceive the total process of singing as
being pyramidal (see illustration on next page.) This concept also describes the order of "events" in vocal production,
and it may help the singer to envision an "outflowing" sensation of the singing process.

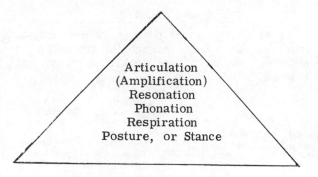

Articulation
(Amplification)
Resonation
Phonation
Respiration
Posture, or Stance

Steps to Achieving Good Posture

The head, chest and pelvis should be supported by the spine in such a way that they align themselves one under the other--head erect, chest high, pelvis rotated so that the "tail is tucked in."

The following "check points" should help the singer to achieve correct posture:

(1) Stand tall (regal) and erect with the feeling that the rib cage is expanded and the body weight is slightly forward on the balls of the feet. There should be a feeling of stretch between the center of the clavicles (the two collar bones, where they join the sternum) and the navel. One foot should be slightly ahead of the other. Avoid spreading the feet too far apart, because that is a clumsy, awkward stance, and it also is not proper posture for aligning the body.

(2) The head should be held high with the chin position being at a 90° angle with the back. One could imagine that a rope, fastened to the top of his head, is gently pulling his head upward in a slightly stretching motion. The posi-

Check Your Carriage Here

In correct, fully erect posture, a line dropped from the ear will go through the tip of the shoulder, middle of hip, back of kneecap, and front of anklebone.

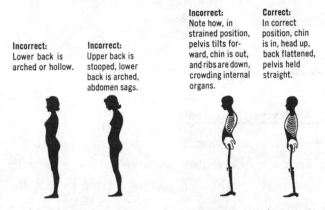

Incorrect:
Lower back is arched or hollow.

Incorrect:
Upper back is stooped, lower back is arched, abdomen sags.

Incorrect:
Note how, in strained position, pelvis tilts forward, chin is out, and ribs are down, crowding internal organs.

Correct:
In correct position, chin is in, head up, back flattened, pelvis held straight.

Figure 36, Correct and Incorrect Posture. (Reproduced by permission of the Schering Corporation.)

---

tion of the head should allow the jaw to be free, not pulled back into the throat. Don't be a "turtle-necked" singer.

(3) Now rotate (see Fig. 36) the base of the spine--in other words, tuck in your pelvis as though you were squeezing sideways through a narrow space. The focal point of muscular tension should be the posterior thigh muscles. I find that when a student successfully achieves this posture and muscular coordination, his stance becomes comfortable. Moreover, with this posture the singer's arms and hands do not feel awkward and thus they assume a natural position at the sides of the body.

(4) Open the throat as though you are about to yawn. (If you do yawn in the process, so much the better to capture the feeling of the openness). Now, inhale a <u>comfortably</u>

To find the correct standing position: Stand one foot away from wall. Now sit against wall, bending knees slightly. Tighten abdominal and buttock muscles. This will tilt the pelvis back and flatten the lower spine. Holding this position, inch up the wall to standing position, by straightening the legs. Now walk around the room, maintaining the same posture. Place back against wall again to see if you have held it.

Figure 37, Improving Incorrect ("Sway-back") Posture. (Reproduced by permission of the Schering Corporation.)

deep, but silent, breath. This is the correct placement of the breath, for it permits the muscles of the abdominal and lumbar (lower back) region to expand as though an innertube were being inflated all around the midriff--back, front and sides, as shown by the Figures 19 and 20 (on pages 56 and 57).

One of the best ways of checking for good posture is to back up against a wall with shoulders, buttocks and heels touching the wall and baseboard respectively. Now place your hand in the "small" of your back. If you find a space there, you have curvature of the spine and you should work to strengthen and coordinate the abdominal and back muscles to correct this malposture. Train yourself vigorously to use your abdominal muscles to flatten your lower abdomen. Whenever you sit, be erect in the chair, tucking in your abdominal muscles--even when riding in an automobile. In time, this muscle contraction will become habitual, thus providing you with the strength to stand comfortably erect!

The "correct" stance at the right in Fig. 36 is quite

rigid. The comfortable stance for singing or walking should be relaxed a bit from this position, especially the shoulders and head. However, the "rotated" pelvis should remain intact.

Another bit of imagery is to visualize a plumb line being dropped down the side of the body. The person with good posture will find that the imaginary plumb line cuts through the middle of the ear, shoulder, hip, knee and ankle bone.

Another check to determine if your posture is correct is to note whether or not your arms and hands feel comfortable at your sides; one should not have to hold them in front, in back, or clasped for security when singing.

An Exercise for the Back and Abdomen

Many persons find it difficult to rotate the pelvis as described above because they have an "acute case" of spinal curvature. Below is another exercise which helps to coordinate and strengthen the abdominal and lower back muscles:

Lie on your back (preferably on a carpeted floor) with heels, calves, buttocks, back of shoulders and head touching the floor.

Tuck in (rotate) the pelvis so that the small of the back touches the floor also, still keeping the knees straight. (If the calves are raised a bit from the floor this does not influence the effectiveness of the exercise as long as the heels are firmly on the floor. The main object is to have the entire spine touch the floor.)

Hold the position until tension is felt across the abdomen and lower back.

Relax and try again. This exercise should be done regularly for two or more periods during the day, so that the abdominal and lower back muscles will gradually strengthen.

132

When these muscles have become sufficiently strength-
ened, practice this exercise in a vertical position when
walking or standing. Again, check yourself by standing with your back against a flat wall with heels,
calves, back and head touching the wall. Then try to
flatten the lower back against the wall surface. It is
interesting to note that, in this standing position,
weight distribution is better balanced; also, one's walk
is smoother when the pelvis is "tucked in." If you
feel rigid, relax the tension a bit, but maintain the
basic stance.

A Summary of Breathing

There are three kinds of breathing in singing:

Clavicular breathing--allowing the chest and shoulders
to heave as most beginners and "pop" singers do. This mode
of breathing is not only inefficient, it does not provide ade-
qute control over exhalation during phonation; and it also
leads to undue throat tension. Rose adds, "if the upper
chest only is used, there is scarcely any tension on the abdominal muscles or diaphragm at the end of inspiration."[1]

Diaphragmatic breathing (intercostal)--expanding principally just below the frontal ribs. This area of concentration of "breath focus" may be identified as rib or costal
breathing; that is, only the thoracic (rib) cage expands.
This action serves the exhalation-phonation process better
than clavicular breathing, but most authorities agree that it
is inadequate for the best control of the "vocal instrument."

Abdominal breathing--expanding in the abdominal region, which exerts pressure against the lower back muscles
and abdominal organs. This style of breathing cannot be
realized to its fullest advantage unless the pelvis is "tucked
in," because the tucking action makes the abdominal muscles
firm. This action, in turn, permits a feeling of lower

133

expansion as though an innertube were being inflated all around that part of the body from inside the singer's pelvic region. This "inflated innertube" feeling should be maintained throughout the entire breath cycle of the phrase to be sung. If the singer will place his hands at the sides of his waist, he will feel this pressure against his fingers and thumbs. This outward expansion should be maintained as though the entire area were an organ wind chest which does not collapse. This breath management is especially helpful in the singer's upper range.

Logically, by incorporating abdominal breathing with the "open throat," breath inhalation is scarcely noticeable. There is no "heaving" for a big breath. Furthermore, breathing in singing should not be considered as a function separate from posture and phonation. Wilson supports this concept in stating:

> It is very important that correct posture be retained during the act of inhalation, that is, shoulders should not be raised, the chest should not cave in, and the abdominal muscles should not collapse and protrude.[2]

Do not be afraid to keep the shoulders high, because, when the pelvis is tucked in (rotated) the shoulders will fall back into a comfortable position.

Wilson provides a further clue as to proper inhalation:

> This condition of inhalation is not possible unless the throat is open for singing. Therefore, the shape of the resonating column must be formed before the breath is taken. The preparation is possible by breathing on the form of the vowel.[3]

If the singer opens his throat in the yawning position as he inhales, the air passage will be open wide enough to facilitate quick, deep and silent breathing. For example, one might think of the vowel "AH" while opening the mouth, and then breathe deeply, but comfortably--not taking in too much air. It should produce the feeling that the chest, diaphragmatic, and abdominal areas of the body are expanding equally to accommodate the over-all expansion of the lungs. In this process of breath management more muscles are used than in either clavicular or diaphragmatic breathing alone. It follows then, if the singer uses his abdominal and lower back muscles, he will achieve better control over his breath. It is to be emphasized that the singer should sustain this expansive feeling throughout the entire breath cycle.

In chest breathing, the muscles around the vocal cords are forced to control the flow of breath, causing excess tension in the vocal mechanism. This improper method of breathing requires the vocal mechanism to be responsible for two functions: first, to phonate, and second to prevent the release of too much breath. Since diaphragmatic breathing also causes some tension in singing, it should be avoided by incorporating the most efficient and effective method of breathing--that of management from the abdominal region.

According to William Vennard, "Correct breathing may be summarized with the three adverbs, 'in, down and out'."[4]

The main principle in breathing is to allow the air to be taken in as freely and comfortably as possible through the mouth and larynx. An especially effective avenue to good breath management is through the concept of the silent breath, which automatically opens the throat for inhalation. Consequently, the silent breath leads to the expansion of the abdominal and lower back muscles and thus, engages the

full component of muscles for "breath control." To achieve
the silent breath inhalation, the singer should simply open the
mouth as though he were about to yawn. Breath will then
enter the lungs noiselessly.

There is no need to emphasize unduly the process of
breath "control." Tedious breathing exercises are a waste
of time. "Breath technique" should and can be applied directly to the singing process. Proper posture, combined with
silent breath inhalation, provides the basic ingredients (and
sensation) for managing the breath during singing. Application of what may be called the "inflated innertube" method of
breathing will provide the singer with the ability to sing longer phrases in one breath, as well as to give better support
to high tones. Beware of "toothpaste tube" breathing--i. e.,
squeezing in; rather, the singer should preserve the expanded
breath support.

The teachers of the bel canto period were known to
admonish the student of voice to start the tone as though
continuing to take a breath. This concept assists the singer
in keeping the muscles of inhalation engaged, so that they
become the "antagonists" of the muscles of exhalation. This
"antagonistic muscle action" is really defining the initial
stage of good breath management. The muscles of inhalation
act as a brake or governor so that the tones can be released
smoothly and evenly.

Finally, clear, clean vowel production will conserve
breath, whereas muddy voweling wastes it.

References

[1]Arnold Rose, The Singer and the Voice (New York: St.
    Martin's Press, 1971), p. 99.

[2]Harry R. Wilson, <u>Artistic Choral Singing</u> (New York: G. Schirmer, 1959), p. 176.

[3]<u>Ibid.</u>

[4]William Vennard, <u>Singing; The Mechanism and the Technic</u> (New York: Carl Fischer, 1967), p. 30.

Chapter VII

AUDIOVISUAL AIDS IN VOICE TEACHING

The Tape Recorder

Strange as it may seem to some readers, many voice teachers often express fear of using the tape recorder for their lessons. This reluctance to use the tape machine stems from a lack of mechanical understanding of the instrument, or from a feeling that it interferes with the sequence of the lesson, or that operating it occupies too much of the lesson time, or that a student is frightened by the sound of his own voice. I am constantly amazed at the number of applied music teachers, who do not take advantage of this teaching technique, which can be so valuable to the learning situation. Currently, there are many good-quality, reasonably-priced machines on the market which are simple to operate by push-button and/or remote control. Improvements in the fidelity of cassette tape recorders have been impressive in recent years, and operation of the machines can be regarded as a valuable instrument in the field of vocal pedagogy. The better quality machines, sold by reputable audio dealers, can be a practical way to record lessons, because the student, himself, can manipulate the recording mechanism from a convenient location and, thus, have a ready means of reference to take with him from the lesson. If desired, cassette tape recorders can be connected to a large reproduc-

tion system which provides a very realistic version of the
singer's efforts. (Normally, the tiny speakers with which
cassette recorders are equipped cannot reproduce a voice
with fidelity. At best, they can illustrate only the obviously
good and bad aspects of the singer's efforts.) If the overall
quality of a particular machine is reasonably good, the reproduction of the voice can be a significant aid to the student
in his own voice analysis.

One great advantage in using a tape recorder is that
it provides immediate feedback of the student's singing--good
or bad. It saves much time in the long run, because the
student and teacher can discuss a given problem with both
of them listening to exactly "what happened"--rather than
trying to recall later what was the specific nature of the problem. The immediacy of the feedback also permits the student
to recall and reinforce the sensation experienced when vocal
production is good.

Moreover, when serious students take their taped lessons with them to use as reference and self-analysis between
sessions, they can learn much from listening and reflection.
Time spent in this manner is far better applied than hours
of "blind" practice, which usually reinforces bad habits.
Critical listening on the part of the student helps him to develop insight into good and bad characteristics of his voice.
If the student can afford several tapes, he can refer to them
occasionally to review his progress and to reinforce comments
made by the teacher. Furthermore, a tape recording of a
voice lesson with an accompanist provides a valuable practice
aid.

This is not to imply that every note should be recorded; nor should the same pattern of recording be followed for

each lesson. Logically, the machine should be adapted to the objectives of the lesson.

Useful Procedures

Select a place to install the equipment which is easily accessible for the operator. If the teacher accompanies lessons himself, it is wise to purchase a reel-to-reel machine with a remote control switch, unless the student uses a cassette. If the instructor has to go to some other part of the room from the location of the piano, naturally, there will be confusion and lost time.

When using a reel-to-reel tape machine, it is advisable to have the tape recorder and microphone more or less permanently set up so that no time is wasted when the machine is operated. (The microphone should be on a stand to achieve maximum fidelity, balance and flexibility of use.) The tape should be advanced to the desired blank place for recording at the beginning of the lesson (preferably by the student). (When purchasing a reel-to-reel recorder, it is advisable to get one that has a "fast forward" and "fast rewind." It will save time and avoid frustration.) A tab of paper can be inserted in the reel to indicate where the tape recorded lesson ended or began. Also, a distance counter gauge is very useful to monitor various segments of the tape.

The microphone should be placed about three to four feet in front of the singer and the recording volume adjusted accordingly to capture as much of the room acoustics as possible. This will produce a recording which sounds essentially the same as the student's original utterance. (Experience will help the teacher to select the correct "mike" position and volume for the particular acoustics of the studio.)

Most tape recorders have "pause" switches or buttons. Use of this component can save tape and time, so the teacher and the student should familiarize themselves with this feature.

There are some very specific advantages to using the tape recorder. Students' vocalises can be recorded to demonstrate to them what they are doing right or wrong as to vowel pronunciation, migration of the vowel on octave skips, and the like (see pages 76 and 79 for some practical vocalises). In recording the student's rendition of a song, stop the machine whenever a significant error is made. Immediately tell the student where and how he erred while reversing the tape to the desired starting place. (Again, experience or a gauge-counter will help the teacher to judge how far back to reverse the tape.) Then, play the tape to illustrate to the student what he has done incorrectly. When the student recognizes his errors and gains insight into his problems from his discussions with his teacher, the phrase should be repeated (and re-recorded) until the desired end is achieved, or at least some insight is made into the problem. The same technique can be used to reinforce something done acceptably or sung very well. (Positive reinforcement is vitally important to the student.)

With advanced vocal students, it is often effective to record an entire song. Then, both teacher and student can listen to it together, stopping the tape where desired, to discuss problems or points of interpretation. The song, or isolated phrases, can be recorded again later for comparison. If the teacher is detained from starting the lesson, the student can begin recording on his own (with or without an accompanist) so that when the teacher arrives, the student's efforts in the teacher's absence can be recaptured.

In voice classes or seminars in which the students perform for each other, the student's song can be recorded, then played back, and finally discussed by the entire group-- referring back to the tape where desired. Choral rehearsals should be recorded so that the members can become part of the critical process, evaluating their collective efforts.

The Visual Medium

A few educational institutions and individuals have videotape machines. These instruments reproduce the visual as well as the audio impressions. (Currently, there is being developed a video-disc machine which records and also plays back inexpensive discs. In time, these machines probably will supersede the more complex and expensive videotape units.) Inasmuch as the visual impression of the singer is very important to the listener in a live performance, and since the singer cannot otherwise "draw back" and observe himself as he performs, visual feedback is an important con- tribution to his self-analysis.

The next best thing to a videotape machine is a full- length mirror in the voice studio and a tape machine of good quality. However, the video-recording machine is the ulti- mate refinement in aiding the student in analyzing his singing and his physical actions (including posture) apart from the moment in which he is preoccupied with his performance. Such a machine permits the student to be more objective than otherwise in attempting to recall what effect his or her physi- cal movements had upon the total performance.

AUDIOVISUAL AIDS

Recitals recorded on audiovisual equipment can be invaluable in analysis as well as for review later in the career of the singer.

Certainly, traumatic elements are present when a singer or choral group listens to their vocal efforts. However, it seems to me that, all too often, singers are unaware of the true sounds which emanate from the vocal organs.

Chapter VIII

ASPECTS OF INTERPRETATION

Any performer should consider his study and eventual
performance of a piece of music to be one of the unique
privileges of life offered him.   Only the composer has more
claim to the music than does the one who attempts to recreate it.   Even so, most composers look to the performer
to literally breathe life into their works.   Therefore, performers have a most important obligation: that of sincerely
and honestly attempting to ascertain what was the composer's
intent.   Inevitably, there will be differences of opinion re-
garding interpretation.   Yet, that obligation is what makes
every performance a challenge.   In the final analysis, the
ultimate control of the voice is through proper interpretation.

Frequently, teachers and singers fall prey to the temp-
tation to believe that when technique is reliable there is little
else about which to be concerned in the performance of a
piece of music.   Instrumentalists, along with choral directors, are equally prone to this fault.   Superior tone quality,
musical accuracy and dynamic contrasts are only prerequisites
to artistic re-creation of the abstract notation of the score.
Realistically, music is nonexistent until it is translated into
organized sound.   Therefore, it behooves the performer to
utilize the musical notation to express his or her interpretation of the work.   Every performing artist should provide at

144

least a slightly different interpretation of the music based upon his own life experience and feelings, and yet, be faithful
to the basic ideas of the composer in terms of style and subtle nuances lying in the music.

Art songs probably represent a composer's truest
feelings as he is inspired by a piece of poetry to provide a
deeper dimension to the text. These pieces require much
more than a mere technical review of the vocal and musical
problems. Surely, these songs require thoughtful reflection
concerning their intent. It should be recognized that a musical performance exposes, however subtly, the performer's
total personality, i.e., the very moment of presentation of a
given song reveals all the insecurities, doubts, fears, sor-
rows, strengths, satisfactions and hopes which have been a
part of the singer's life experiences. That is what makes
live performances exciting!

Songs are the most personal expressions of any composer and, thus, they deserve the most careful respect and
study during their preparation for performance.

It is mandatory, therefore, for every singer to reflect upon the text of a song in terms of his own sense of
the meaning. The singer should spend a great deal of time
going over the thoughts and words, their inflections and inner
meanings, and then reapply them to the musical thoughts.
After becoming familiar with a song as a whole, it is extremely valuable for the singer to study and recite the words
out of context of the music itself to determine the flow of the
textual syntax: where the natural inflections occur. If the
text and music seem incompatible to the singer as he re-
flects upon the matter, possibly the music is not valid (at
least for him or her), or the text may be an awkward trans-

lation of a foreign language. In either case the music should be abandoned after the singer has satisfied him- or herself that the music and text have little in common.

Composer Dominick Argento stated in an address to the 1976 convention of the National Association of Teachers of Singing, "there is no place to hide. The composer appears almost naked to us in his songs and, likewise, the singer."[1]

Therefore, it behooves every singer to establish on his own terms what the composer and author are attempting to say, while still remaining true to the notation. Operatic arias, especially, should never be studied without an understanding of the opera's plot and the specific place and meaning of the aria within the story. Likewise, a thorough translation, word by word, should be made by the singer. Fortunate is the singer who also fluently speaks and understands the foreign language in which he is singing.

Breathing and Interpretation

The breath punctuation in singing is of utmost importance to interpretation of a song. I am appalled at the number of singers who pay little or no heed to breathing as a part of poetic punctuation. The breath is an integral part of the musical intent of a song. If the text and music are incompatible as to breathing, the mismarriage calls for an annulment.

In strophic songs, such as we encounter in folk songs and hymns, the textual punctuation usually does not conform to the musical phrase in succeeding verses after the first one. Therefore, it behooves the singer to treat the text and music carefully in order to maintain the integrity of both of these elements.

Unsupported Tones Can Affect Interpretation

Many singers produce a large percentage of excellent tones, but still allow a significant number of others to be lacking in vitality. These "dead fish" tones destroy the beauty of a lovely legato phrase line. They occur often on short notes and short vowels such as the derivative and modified vowels (see Vowel Spectrum, page 69). These un-resonant tones can occur also on any vowel, depending upon the sequence in a song.

A legato phrase requires <u>tonal vitality on every note</u> in order to sustain the intended meaning. Since Handel's Messiah has been used previously and is familiar to so many persons, the examples in Fig. 38 should be helpful in illustrating this point.

The circled notes are the unsupported "dead fishes" so often heard, even by well-established altos and sopranos. Most of these singers have developed solid breath management, so the lack of tonal support cannot necessarily be caused by faulty breath management. Rather, the cause of these dead tones stems from lack of vowel support, i. e., a weakly produced vowel. Note in the following illustration that the unsupported tones occur on notes of shortest duration, whereby they are susceptible to being "thrown away." These two arias are fraught with such traps, as are most songs with compound meters. Strophic songs also pose these problems of uneven tone production because, almost every note of the piece contains a different vowel sound; thus, every short

147

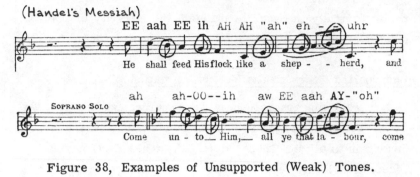

Figure 38, Examples of Unsupported (Weak) Tones.

---

note is vulnerable to this neglect of uniform tone quality throughout a given phrase. Consonants that are not "in line" with the vowel can cause weak or unfocused vowel production--thus weakening the tone on that particular note.

Solution: Clearly defined vowels, focused well-forward and supported by the expansive type of breath management described in Chapter VI. This is the application of vocal technique to expressive singing.

Certainly, this description is not meant to encourage stodgy, metronomic singing! There must be nuances and stresses throughout so that the phrase develops to its apex and then releases. Any musical phrase must have horizontal drive; it must "go somewhere." Simple folk songs, art songs and recitatives are the types of songs most prone to uneven tone quality and uninteresting phrasing. Every note, stressed or unstressed should be vital (energized) unless produced for a special effect of expression.

In reference to the horizontal drive of the music, it should be noted that, all too often, musical phrases are vertically conceived, even in staccato singing. That is to say, that when most of the technical aspects of a song are realized, the music lacks interest beyond the fact that the mechanical conditions have been mastered to a significant degree. (Choral singing is particularly susceptible to this fault.) Dynamic contrasts are merely a means of diagraming a piece of music. Musical dynamics should emerge from textual relationships and, consequently, the flow of words should unite the contrasting elements of expression. Meaningful recitation of the words out of context of the music is the best means of gaining insight into the composer's intent. The emotional quality of the spoken word provides the basic dramatic spirit of the vocal tones to be produced.

Musical Style

Every singer should strive to be an artist, regardless of his technical ability. What I mean by that statement is that every student of singing should also study basic musical styles so that he does not sing Baroque period music in the same fashion as he would sing Romantic music. The singer should recognize that Mozart's music is different from J. S. Bach's, even though there are some similarities in their styles. Many operatic singers I have auditioned for my Bach Festival concerts have disappointed me in that they sing Baroque arias in the same fashion as they perform Verdi and Puccini arias. So-called "contemporary music" has such a wide variety of styles that one cannot categorize it as one would do for music through the Impressionistic period, so one must consider carefully the subtleties in style required by the particular piece of this modern era. In-depth exploration of musical periods would require at least the perusal of great volumes of material and is out of the realm of many singing students, but basic familiarity with various musical styles, including vocal textures, should be mandatory for every singer. Vocal instructors should be well acquainted with the important differences among singing styles so as to be able to coach the student on styles as well as technique.

If one performs with true understanding of the style and texture of the music, he or she must "get behind" the music and not use it as a vehicle to "show off" technique and vocal beauty. Frequently, a performance of a song may appear to be such that the vocalist is singing to himself--expressing the totality of the music for his own benefit, the audience being allowed to eavesdrop. However, there are occasions in which one might well "entertain" his or her audience when singing a humorous song or a selection which gives advice to the listener.

If one's own emotional understanding of a song is clear, the emotions of an audience can be aroused through the sincerity of the interpretation. The interpretation should stem from an inner conception of the music. "Simple" songs are frequently overlooked as having deep intrinsic meanings. For instance, "Drink To Me Only With Thine Eyes" is a difficult piece to express adequately. First, it is a very familiar song and most listeners subconsciously follow the continuity. Second, it is another example of songs susceptible to unsupported ("dead fish") tones, which threaten the gracefulness of the beautiful legato phrases. Third, the climax of each phrase needs to be considered very carefully, applying word-emphases to the musical phrases. Finally, there must be deep emotion present in the expression of the textual and musical content without becoming "slushy" or overly sentimental about it. In short, this "simple" song is really a very difficult selection to perform, if one is to be sincere about its subtleties.

The Performance

The preparation of a musical program requires more than being secure in the technical and expressive aspects of the material to be presented. Performers should "psych" themselves for the performance (ideally) by being certain to be rested and fresh for the appearance. Any "worrying" should be done long before one steps out onto the stage.

The singer needs to anticipate in advance of a performance everything that relates to him and to his audience.

Gracious stage deportment from the moment of entry until the singer and his accompanying forces disappear, are crticially important to the total satisfaction of the audience and performers. Many excellent, artistic performances have been marred by an ungracious or clumsy performer. Gestures should be natural and subtle, always within the mood of the song. Moreover, redundant gestures become boring and distracting to the audience. Any hand, arm or body movements must come from a natural feeling to add this subtle "third dimension" to the music.

The order of stage entry is very important in the establishing of proper stage etiquette, so that a song recital can begin with grace and dignity. Normally, the soloist enters first, assuredly and quickly, with his piano accompanist following, both bowing slightly to acknowledge applause, providing the performers are of the same sex or the singer is female and the accompanist is male. If the singer is

151

male and the accompanist female, the accompanist should
enter first with the male singer following closely behind.
On a large stage, they may possibly enter together, each
going to his selected place for the bow. In every situation
the woman should enter and leave first.

When a soloist is accompanied by a small group or an
orchestra, the accompanying artists should enter first and
tune up; all physical requirements of seating, stands, etc.
being set up in advance by a stage hand. When the accom-
panists have become silent, the artist should enter immediately. Few things are more annoying to an audience than
having a long delay before the artist arrives on stage. Therefore, the ensemble should never enter the stage unless the
artist has informed the leader that he or she is ready to
enter also. When an ensemble conductor is involved, the
conductor follows the soloist on stage after the tuning.

In response to the applause which usually greets
performers, the bow should consist of only a slight bending
of the upper part of the body from the torso. A pleasant
smile (not a grin) should accompany this response to the
audience.

When everyone has become quiet and receptive, (and
only then) should the singer indicate to his accompanist(s)
to begin the introduction to his first selection. The signal
to the accompanist need not be obvious. A glance at the
pianist or group leader is usually sufficient. Then begin to
sing with confidence. It is extremely important for the artist to instruct his ushers before the performance that no
one is to be seated during any song.

Always remain in the mood of the music during instru-
mental introductions and interludes. That portion of a song

is just as important as the measures which are sung.

If a performer makes a mistake of any kind, he should not wince or indicate to the audience that he knows that he "goofed." If he becomes completely lost, and it is obvious that he cannot continue, he should look at his accompanist for a cue, or quietly go over to the piano and look at the score. If he is being accompanied by several performers, very likely they will continue to play and he should, then, enter when he is able to.

For the most part, when bowing between selections in a series of songs which comprise a recital "song group," acknowledge the applause conservatively with only a slightly deeper bow than the opening bow. Once again, a smile usually is in order. A song cycle should not be interrupted by applause, and, consequently, the singer's mood and expression should remain through the concluding accompaniment of the song, changing only when the introduction of the next song begins, or when the song begins without accompaniment.

At the conclusion of the song group, the singer should bow once graciously and then gesture to his accompanist(s) to stand. Then, all should bow together once again and the soloist should immediately leave the stage with the same dispatch with which he or she entered. It is of utmost importance that performers avoid dawdling on the stage after they have concluded a segment of a concert or recital. The audience becomes embarrassed at being obligated to continue its applause, or the performers become embarrassed because they must "retreat" in silence.

If applause does not diminish after the performers have left the stage, the soloist should return immediately to a prominent place on the stage (not necessarily to his performance spot) to acknowledge the continued appreciation. Again, don't delay; just bow graciously and walk quickly off the stage again. It cannot be over-emphasized that getting on and off the stage quickly (but with dignity) is of utmost importance.

One final word about a recital performance is important to consider. One must pace oneself throughout the entire recital. Always save a little bit of emotion and energy for yourself. Know that you could give a little more than you exhibit. Never "bleed to death" before the audience. Also, the artist must recognize that room acoustics invariably change from when it is empty to when it is full of people. Therefore, the texture of the sound will be different, and consequently, the singer may experience a strange, "deserted" feeling. He or she should anticipate this change in acoustics and rely upon solid technique and inspiration to compensate for previous rehearsal experience in the hall. The performer must have faith that the audience will hear a fuller sound than seems to be the case at the time.

Reference

[1]Dominick Argento, "The Composer and the Singer," NATS Bulletin 33:3 (May 1977), 21.

Chapter IX

IN SUMMATION

I   General Hints on Singing

The problem of semantics emphasizes how difficult it
is for one person to tell another in writing exactly what to
do to improve his vocal production. Terms and words often
conjure up images in others that differ from our own, and
not every suggestion can be applied to all individuals under
the same circumstances. Therefore, the student must strive
to interpret a teacher's or writer's comments in view of his
own growing perceptions--not just believing blindly or "par-
roting" their remarks.

For the most part, descriptions of the technique of
singing are subjective and intangible because the "instrument"
cannot be seen. Moreover, when we become overly analyti-
cal and "scientific" in our teaching efforts, we tend to lose
the instinctive nature that must be developed by every singer
as he builds his technique and improves his "instrument."
All other instruments are finished products before the player
operates them; the singer must develop and refine his "instrument" as he matures musically. The vocalist must train
his mind to coordinate 130 working parts of his body in the
act of singing. There must be freedom from muscular tension; yet the muscles must be firm. The singer must control
his breath, both intake and release. He must also train his

mind to identify specific vocal sounds so that his voweling becomes exact and flexible. Moreover, he must learn to "feel" what is the proper sensation as well as listening to his vocal production.

Phrasing is extremely important and should be regarded as the essential means by which the text is interpreted (communicated) to the listener. Sometimes the musical phrases must be subordinated to the textual phrases if the latter is stronger in emphasis, such as often happens in strophic songs--(lieder, hymns or ballads). Incorrect phrasing is inexcusable and indicates that the singer is not concentrating upon the meaning of the text. If a text is awkward to sing, the composer may have been indifferent to the rhythm of the words, or it may be a bad translation of a text originally composed in another language. In such instances, it behooves the student and the teacher to consider seriously whether or not the song merits the effort which must be expended upon it.

The carrying power (projection) of pianissimo tones depends largely upon how well they are focused and energized. These soft tones demand that the singer give even more attention to precise vowel focus than he would in producing fortissimo tones. The "forward focus" of tonal sensation utilizes the higher partials of the tone--thus providing the necessary resonance to project these soft tones.

II Six Basic Principles for the Aspiring Singer

(1) There must be a sincere desire to improve the voice.

(2) It must be recognized that physical vitality is demanded
   of every singer. Therefore, one must keep physically

fit at all times in order to perform at one's best.

(3) <u>Concentration</u> and <u>mental discipline</u> need to be developed.
This is difficult to achieve, when there are so many
"things" to think about during the act of singing. That
is why vocal technique must become almost automatic
in the singer's development and why this pragmatic
approach to singing via vowel production is advanced.
<u>Daily practice sessions</u> will aid greatly in the develop-
ment of discipline. A specific time in the daily rou-
tine must be arranged for vocal study. The practice
schedule format should be carefully planned. <u>Always</u>
<u>have an overall goal in mind</u> as well as minor objec-
tives toward which to work, even though the goals and
objectives may not be reached during a given session.
<u>Rest periods are very important.</u> The student should
pace himself according to his physical and mental
endurance; <u>avoid exhausting practice.</u> Resting from
the act of singing can be utilized to study the theoreti-
cal aspects of the music, or to memorize it. Time
is well-spent just <u>thinking</u> about the act of singing,
and most certainly listening to a tape recording which
has been made in the studio lesson, or at a practice
session. Certainly, analyzing one's own singing on
tape is more profitable than practicing without purpose
or understanding of one's problems.

(4) The singer must recognize that <u>correct voweling</u> (shaping
of the oral pharynx) is the basis of all tone production.
Clean (pure) voweling is the first concept to master
in singing. Unsupported tones are almost invariably
caused by the absence of vowel focus (malformed
vowels).

(5) Breathing must be coordinated with voweling (tone production) during the act of singing.

(6) Forward resonance must be achieved in singing by means of spoken projection. This "extended speech" concept assists greatly in achieving proper resonance. "Say it, then sing it" along the track of the spoken voice, adding the necessary space for proper amplification of vocal sound.

III Specific Axioms for Singers

(1) DICTION: Diction is the means by which proper vocal production is achieved. Phonation and diction cannot be separated from each other. Therefore, the exact communication of the words of a song in any language must be clearly understood. Otherwise, one produces tone and then tries to clear up the diction--an almost impossible task, because the process is backwards. The manner in which the singer speaks the words as he sings largely determines his tone quality, vocal timbre and voice placement.

(2) FOCUS: The contour of the oral pharynx provides the character of each vowel. Every vowel has its particular size and shape on every pitch, and consequently, tonal focus is the result of proper vowel production. The student should not be afraid of "frontal focus." Some singers describe it as a "buzzing" in the mask. Here again, the student, listening to his rehearsal and lesson tapes, can coordinate his "inner hearing" with the desired end of tone production. This need to develop a proper aural image of the overall timbre of one's voice is one of the most important facets of singing. What seems to be a nasal sound as a person sings is usually

not that at all if he elevates the soft palate enough to add the proper depth and height to the tones produced.

(3) VOWELS: (a) All vowels must be "deeply set" and carefully formed through the shaping of the oral pharynx. Diffused vowels produce weak or breathy tones because of wasted breath. Over-sized vowels produce "woofy" (dark) tones. Moreover, accurate conception of all vowels in the singer's mind produces amazing results in achieving efficiency of the vocal mechanism. (b) All subordinate "ah" sounds should be modified toward the "father" AH sound. (See Vowel Spectrum, page 69.) (c) Small vowels beget small tones. However, one must keep in mind constantly that the respective vowels differ in size, and that everything is relative. On the other hand, do not over-form any vowel lest the "forward focus" (ping) be lost. Do make room in the oral pharynx, but always within the confines of the correct vowel formation in relation to the height of the pitch.

(4) CONSONANTS: Consonants must always be "in line" with the vowel; that is to say, that the velum must never be permitted to collapse when pronouncing consonants in the upper range of the voice. The consonant must be less percussive ("softened") as the tone ascends, so as not to constrict the throat; or, to state it another way, the consonant must correspond with the size of the vowel.

(5) INTONATION: Intonation can be improved through vowel focus. It is the process by which the singer combines a blend of higher and lower partials (formants) of the particular vowel (tone) on a given pitch. This combination of higher and lower partials provides the total ingredients which form both vitality and roundness of tone quality throughout the scope of the vocal range. Vocal flexibility and clarity

of diction are also enhanced by proper vowel focus.

(6) TONE COLOR: Tone color, as a concept, is governed by the manner in which the singing words are "spoken." Frequently, the singer should excerpt the words from the song and speak them with the desired emphasis; intoning them, as it were. The spoken tones should be sustained as much as possible in the basic rhythm of the musical symbols. Poetry should be read aloud expressively. Monotone recitation is of no value at all. Expressive reading of a text gives the singer clues of emphasis and de-emphasis for application of the text to the musical phrases. Then, the words should be re-introduced into the songs keeping in mind the concept that singing is really an extension of speech. The vowels determine the character of the tones to be produced. Words come first--before the tone is produced.

(7) THE "YAWN": The purpose of the slight yawning sensation is to lift the soft palate slightly (with the nostrils slightly flared) but not so much that the vowel is malformed. The slight yawn creates the necessary space for amplification of the tone, and "connects" the breath with the tone. However, one must always project the tone (vowel) "forward" in the mask to avoid "throaty" or "woofy" tone quality.

(8) THE NARROW CHANNEL: One should always conceive of (imagine) the tone traveling in a narrow channel as the pitches rise so as to avoid "spreading" or diffusing the vowel (and thus the tone), particularly during a melisma or any vocal line which "travels" on a single vowel sound.

(9) BREATHING: THE "TWO-WAY STRETCH": This feeling is achieved, during inhalation, by employing the slight yawn (lift of the soft palate), and at the same time allowing

the descending diaphragm to press down against the abdominal organs. This action exerts pressure all around the
abdomen; the "inflated innertube" sensation. The development
of this two-way stretch has proven to me to be one of the
most significant skills in singing: firm support of the vowel
in the buccalpharyngeal cavity and abdominal support from
below. They seem to go in different directions, but they
really "connect" in the total process of singing.

(10) RELEASE OF THE JAW: Jaw tension causes
shrill or harsh tones, particularly in the upper range of the
voice. Furthermore, jaw tension prevents the vocal musculature from making proper adjustments as the voice crosses
the passaggio. Therefore, one should release the jaw while
simultaneously giving special attention to forward vowel focus.
One means of accomplishing this objective is to imagine
(while singing) that the jaw is suspended on rubber bands,
and that it "follows" the contour of vowel shape of the soft
and hard palates.

IV Visible Faults

(1) "Bobbling" larynx (larynx movement up and down) may be
    caused by unequal tension among the muscles in the
    laryngeal area and/or faulty control of breath. Con-
    centrate upon more accurate voweling with special
    attention given to attaining a more forward production.
    Then, refer your concentration to achieving solid
    breath control; the objective being to connect tone
    production with breath management.

(2) The raised larynx is usually caused by lack of the slight
    yawn feeling, faulty intake of air (throat restriction

during inhalation), and/or a lifted chin. Check your
posture with a mirror to determine that your body
alignment is correct. (See Chapter VI.) To determine laryngeal movement, either up or down, place
a finger in the notch of the larynx when singing. This
experiment will show you whether or not your larynx
is in a low, medium or high position as you sing.
Swallowing will raise the larynx and a full yawn will
lower it considerably.

(3) The lowered larynx also can be a problem, i.e., when
it is excessively low in the throat. This condition
is caused by too much yawn in the oral pharynx. Invariably, a "woofy" tone results from this kind of
malformation. Concentrate upon a smaller vowel formation (size and shape) for the particular height of
the pitch. Proper vowel formation will produce a
better blending of higher and lower partials of the
tone as well as allow the larynx to assume a more
moderate position.

(4) When the back of the tongue is tight or curled up at its
tip and away from the teeth ("ski-jump" formation),
a throaty, "dark" tone is produced. Work toward
establishing a tongue position that is low in the floor
of the mouth and reasonably far forward on all vowels;
for instance, a concave tongue shape on the vowel
"AH. "

(5) The trembling jaw, caused by unequal tension between the
vocal musculature and the jaw, is a common fault in
singing. Release (let go of) jaw tension and concentrate upon accurate vowel formation. Again, imagine
the jaw to be suspended by rubber bands.

(6) The protruding jaw occasionally may be the result of
an occluded jaw--a physical abnormality with which
one is born and which only surgery can alleviate.
Sometimes, oral braces can alter the bite to bring the
lower jaw into a more correct relationship with the
upper teeth and thus relieve the tension caused by the
malfunctioning bite. In more minor cases of protruding jaw, the malady can be cured by helping the student to achieve complete release of jaw tension (as in
III, 10 above, page 161).

(7) "Tucking in" the chin is sometimes caused by overcom-
pensation to cure lifting the chin: "turtle neck" position. Check posture in front of a mirror for body
alignment. Be certain that the rib cage is high and
the buttocks are "tucked in." (See pages 130-131.)

(8) Singers with non-active lips (tense jaws and tongues)
should concentrate upon more precise enunciation of
the words. Be certain that the lips are free of muscular tension. One should be able to "purse the lips"
slightly on most vowels without impeding tone production, if the lips are free of tension, but not "flabby."

(9) The grinning smile (Cheshire cat grin) causes shallow
tone and muscular tension throughout the vocal mechanism, including the lips. This is an external (and
incorrect) attempt to gain brightness in the tone and
to achieve "forward" production. The smile (or grin)
often causes the tone to spread. Rather, forward
production can be achieved by relaxing the lift of the
soft palate just a bit, being certain to confine the
vowel to a narrow "channel" behind the upper front
teeth and hard palate by means of the "sneer" or

"snarl." Care must be exercised so that the combination of "forward thrust" and lift of the soft palate is achieved.

(10) Opening the front of the mouth too widely closes the throat. The spatial relationship between the mouth opening and the buccalpharyngeal cavity should be governed by vowel clarity; this in relation to the depth needed for proper amplification of the tone.

(11) If the chest and shoulders are raised too high and are rigid, concentrate on rotating the pelvis as in item 12 immediately below. "Tuck in" the pelvic region, but be careful not to rotate the pelvis so far that erect posture is disturbed (See Chapter VI). Pelvic rotation assists in releasing shoulder and chest tension. However, be certain not to "list" backward when "tucking in" the pelvis, or to permit the rib cage to drop. Be sure that the body weight is forward on the balls of the feet.

(12) The protruding abdomen indicates bad posture and weak back muscles. When this condition exists, the student should work on "tucking in" the pelvis while simultaneously holding the rib cage high. Stand against the wall with heels against the baseboard. Then, try to flatten out the small of the back against the wall; or lie on the floor and "dig in" with the heels (see Chapter VI, concerning exercises for the back and abdomen).

V Audible Faults

(1) Gasping or noisy breath inhalation can be cured by

"opening the throat" (the slight yawn effect) permitting silent breath inhalation. Remedy: Do not suck in breath. Rather, breath inhalation should be unnoticed.

(2) Breathing in general: not having enough breath for average phrases indicates that breath is being wasted through lack of control of the muscles governing exhalation and phonation. Many singers mistakenly believe that they must take "big breaths" for long (and/or loud) passages and "small breaths" for short (and/or soft) passages. On the contrary, it is rather how the breath is taken in (inhaled) and how it is released (exhaled--efficiency of breath management during the process of phonation) that governs so-called "breath control": "the tone controls the breath.... The pure vowel will not waste breath."[1] Do you have a feeling of expansion around the entire mid-section? Along with pure voweling, the sensation should be analogous to an inner-tube being inflated inside the waist line. The diaphragm is like an inverted saucer which moves down and flattens out at full inhalation. The lungs should be filled by way of the silent breath, keeping the rib-cage high and the pelvis tucked in. This process employs all of the lower abdominal and dorsal muscles for proper breath management. The muscles of inhalation should press the abdominals against the viscera, thus displacing the space where the air was. This acts as a control valve to keep the air from rushing out too quickly. This is what is really meant by "breath control."

(3) The tremelo (wobbly tone), is usually caused by faulty breath management, unequal muscular tension in the throat, or the larynx dropped too low (too much yawn). Remedy: To alleviate this condition, the singer must achieve a more forward focus, thus raising the larynx slightly from

its depressed position.

(4) The bleat (excessively thin, uneven vibrato, the opposite of the tremolo) is caused by uneven tension in the vocal musculature (the "tight throat"). Remedy: Concentrate upon releasing the jaw and tongue of all tension and add a bit of the yawning feeling, thus lowering the larynx slightly.

(5) Poor Intonation is usually caused by lack of concentration and/or poor control of the breath and/or poor voweling. Remedy: Every note should be energized. There should be no "flabby" tones in the singer's production which cause the pitch to flat. Keep all vowels highly arched (focused) behind the upper front teeth on the hard palate so that there will be enough high partials in the tone to make the sound bright. These higher partials in the tone tend to correct flatting, because the ear tends more readily to hear these higher formants of the particular vowel. Sharping is usually caused by undue tension in the vocal musculature, usually the jaw. Remedy: Concentrate on releasing any jaw or neck tension by yawning and by employing various relaxation exercises for the neck. Then re-employ some of the yawn as you sing, probably more than you think you need.

(6) The Attack: (a) Is it breathy, allowing too much air to escape through the vocal cords before they phonate fully? Remedy: Concentrate on vowel production, being certain to be absolutely accurate in vowel articulation before the attack.

(b) Do you slide into the vowel via the consonant? Remedy: Get to the vowel as quickly as possible, but be certain that the position of the oral pharynx during the formation of the consonant is "in line" with the vowel. Consonants cannot sustain a pitch by themselves--only liquid consonants (sub-vowels) and vowels can do that. Also concentrate upon hearing the exact pitch mentally before singing it.

(c) Is there a glottal stroke (explosion of the tone)? Remedy: Concentrate upon coordinating the formation of the consonant with the vowel which immediately follows it. "Sigh" into the tone while envisioning proper production.

(7) "Classically" incorrect types of tone: (7a) Throaty, two types: the first is the pinched, tight, "necktie tenor" piercing sound. Remedy: practice achieving a slight yawning sensation while singing. If the chin is lifted and tight, release the jaw; permit it to find its natural level. The jaw should "follow"--not lead, and it should be freely suspended as though hanging on rubber bands. The second is the overly-dark, "woofy" tone caused by overformed vowels (an exaggerated formation). Remedy: Concentrate upon smaller vowel formation--correct relationship between the oral pharynx (throat) and front of mouth. Be certain that the vowel is clearly "focused" behind the upper front teeth.

(7b) Nasal tone (reedy, buzzy) caused by lack of "lift" of the soft palate (oral pharynx)--the soft palate not being raised enough and/or constriction in the oral and naso-pharynx. This tone production is not basically incorrect. Rather, it is incomplete. Remedy: Concentrate on achieving more "lift" (slight yawning feeling) while still maintaining the forward focus as experienced in the nasal tones. The proper coordination of forward focus and slight yawn provides the singer with the proper formants required for the respective pitches he desires to sing.

(7c) "White" (blatant-shallow) tone is often identified with nasal, thin tone. Remedy: Concentrate upon more "deeply-set" vowels achieved via the slight yawning feeling and low tongue position.

(8) Poor diction is usually caused by weak consonants, unfocused vowels, or "woofy," dark vowels. Some clues to this malady are: (8a) Sluggish initial or final consonants. Remedy: Consonants should always be "in-line" with the vowel next to it. (8b) Anticipating or prolonging final consonants (usually "sub-vowels"). For instance, "migrating" from the vowel toward the consonant or diphthong too soon as in such words as "still" (stih-lll), "sight" (sah-eet), etc., are some causes for poor diction. Remedy: Maintain the pure vowel throughout the duration of the note value. (8c) Mixing dual sounds (diphthongs), that is, allowing sounds which vanish as in "say" (sAY-ee), "go" (gOH-oo), etc., results in muddy diction. Remedy: Avoid diphthong migration.

(8d) Improper use of "r" sound often impairs vocal production. There are three kinds of remedy. First, the Italian "r" (rolled or trilled on the front of the tongue) frees the tongue from tension and the hard "r" sound. Young children often produce the Italian "r" when they attempt to imitate the sound of a car engine as they play with toys. When needed, I ask the male singer who says he cannot roll or trill his tongue to recreate the "toy car motor" sound. This sometimes aids in the achievement of frontal tongue action. However, some persons cannot "trill" with the tongue, usually because the oral frenulum is too thick. Second, for difficulties with medial tongue action, soften the roll--or "flip" the "r." This is done by allowing the tongue to "flip up" behind the upper front teeth as the sound is completed.

168

IN SUMMATION

Third, the final soft "r" should finish a word, using the concept of the "uhr" (see Vowel Spectrum, page 69).

VI The Passaggio

The passaggio encompasses the several notes surrounding the "break" in the untrained voice. The voice can break at several different pitches, depending upon how far the singer forces his voice upward. This "register transition" demands that the singer imagine the lighter sound of the falsetto or "head voice" below the "break" so as to introduce a lighter approximation of the vocal folds, simultaneously incorporating some of the heavier production (from the lower voice) as the voice rises just above the "break." (See Chapter IV.) This "thinning of the mass" provides a more even quality between the "head" and "chest" voices. The singer should concentrate upon producing a pure vowel and a released jaw at this point to permit the vocal mechanism to function more naturally and efficiently. It should be emphasized that one should imagine both vocal colors--the heavier (chest) production and the falsetto or head voice simultaneously. (I term the process the "stereo effect.") One more admonition to be reasserted is that the singer should take particular care not to overform the vowel in this area of his tessitura. Smaller, careful formation of the oral pharynx over the passaggio is imperative!

Finally, the placement of vowel focus should always be felt behind the front teeth--in the forward section of the hard palate; yet with enough arching of the soft palate to give depth to the tone. The vowel focus should never "fall" to the floor of the mouth.

The passaggio problem requires great patience on the part of both the aspiring singer and the teacher. The method of attack upon the problem for singers with this break or yodeling action is two-fold--mental and physical:

MENTAL: Singers must realize that the vocal "break" is a common muscular-coordination problem among tenors, baritones and basses as well as with most mezzos and altos. If a "break" is present, the student and teacher cannot afford to ignore it. The solution to the "break" requires an undetermined amount of time, though usually a great deal, to establish muscular coordination and added strength so that the muscles governing production in the upper vocal range (which are naturally weak from lack of use) can function effectively enough to "bridge" the lower and upper ranges of the voice. Much of this development depends upon the ability of the singer to have an aural image of the tone quality he or she must produce.

The singer must first learn to "thin-out" the vocal mass of the "chest voice" as he approaches his passaggio, thus achieving a less heavy approximation of the vocal bands. This permits the "chest" and "head" voices to resemble each other in timbre (the "stereo effect"). Again, this requires concentration of the singer to imagine the desired tone quality (aural image) before the note is sung. The net result should be that the transition from the lower to upper range of the voice will be achieved more evenly. The singer must "live with" and use a weaker sound of the supported falsetto until his musculature develops the strength and coordination necessary to employ the vocal mechanism correctly.

PHYSICAL: Begin singing softly in the supported

falsetto range (see page 118) about three or four notes above
the "break" on the vowel "OO" (or humming without tension),
striving for complete release of all muscular tension in the
lips and jaw.   This practice serves to strengthen the vocal
muscles in the upper range of the voice.   The freely-produced
hum in the upper voice is the basic approximation of the vocal
bands for singing in the upper regions of the voice.   After
establishing an acceptable tone ("OO" is a very small vowel
and one should be extremely careful not to over-form it in
the high range), descend slowly down below the "break" in
the supported falsetto position as far as the singer can go.
(Some singers can carry the lighter position down as much
as an octave below the "break" by keeping the soft palate in
a raised position--thus avoiding the "chest voice" entirely.
Continue this exercise until the passaggio becomes free of
"switching gears."   Then, gradually go to higher starting
pitches above the passaggio as the ability to sing successfully
down across the "break" is experienced.   Also, gradually
increase the volume of the tone.   Finally, reverse the procedure, being certain to "lighten" up the tone quality as the
voice approaches the passaggio.   Do not despair that the tone
is weak at this point.   Rather, strive for vowel focus--a
pure "OO" sound, alternating with humming, before attempting other vowels over the same series of notes.

    Work specifically for a "forward" focus, again being
certain that the lips are free of tension; the "OO" vowel is
pure and not over-formed (overformation of it produces a
heavy, "woofy" tone and a thick approximation of the vocal
bands); the action of the abdominal method of breathing is
employed to support the tones.   Gradually utilize all vowel
sounds in this falsetto position, but add a slight "snarl" or

"sneer" with the lips. When vowel focus (placement) becomes secure, concentration on the "snarl" or "sneer" can be relaxed. This position of the lips serves only to gain focus and must not be allowed to go to the extreme of facial contortion. The "snarl" or "sneer" can be adapted easily to the singing of songs. It is not, necessarily, just a vocalise. (See Chapter IV for other details.)

Patience and long suffering, combined with accurate voweling, supported by proper breath management, are means of solving the "problem of the break." Eventually, there should be no "break" in the voice; the ideal should be a smooth transition throughout the entire scope of the vocal range.

VII The Falsetto

The falsetto may be classified into two kinds: the "collapsed" or breathy type and the "supported" type. In the former, the vocal folds are so lightly approximated that the thyroarytenoid muscles are very nearly passive, whereas the tone in the supported falsetto (though light in timbre) is dynamically flexible, engaging some action of the arytenoid muscles.

My experience has been that the supported falsetto can be achieved through the "snarl" or "sneer" feeling (a very forward "placement" of the tone) in this vocal zone, rather than focused back in the oral pharynx.

Some singers have a "natural" bridge from the lower to upper range of their voices. My interpretation of this phenomenon is that these vocalists instinctively are able to thin out the "mass" of the vocal folds to make the transition smooth. This leads us back to the "passaggio problem," a very frustrating experience for many male singers, especially tenors, who often must sing across this area of their range. Sometimes they must sing in the tessitura from e to g above middle c for long phrases at mezzoforte to fortissimo dynamics. Therefore, they should conceive of pure vowels with a concept of intensity of tone (no matter what dynamic level is required), rather than developing an aural image of heavy vocal production. The analogy of a rifle bullet versus a shotgun blast may be applied to singing: the vocal tone should be stripped of its "fat," which spreads and cannot carry a great distance. Rather, the tone should be well-focused like the rifle bullet, which carries farther with more impact and uses less powder. Such a tone, produced by clear, efficient voweling, projects far and uses less breath energy.

VIII The Lips

The position of the lips can also affect vowel formation. For instance, a weakly-shaped "OO" or "OH" lip position invariably produces a weak and diffused tone. "Lazy lips" tend to produce diffused tones. The lips should form the final shaping of the vowel, sometimes referred to as "rounding off" the vowel. Conversely, the singer should avoid the "stiff upper lip" in singing. The tension caused by the lips readily transfers to the other muscles involved in the neck and throat.

One of the most preposterous outrages inflicted upon the world of vocal pedagogy is the publishing of pictures of how every individual's lips should be formed on a given vowel. Common sense will refute this notion if one considers that some individual's teeth protrude more than others, some mouths are very large and wide (or some very small and narrow), some persons are thick-lipped and other thin-lipped, etc. (This is one reason so many young singers go astray; they imitate rather than emulate their favorite teacher's or singing idol's facial and mouth mannerisms). Moreover, unification of vowel sounds should come from the recognition that each individual's "architecture" must provide the structure for the formation of the vowel sound which he should accurately produce. Therefore, unification of vowel sounds should come from the basic concept that each person's most natural lip and mouth formations should be utilized.

IX Voice Classification

The process of voice classification is a controversial one. Vocal timbre is one obvious means of establishing classification. However, depending upon the aural image which the singer has of his own voice, that person might well darken or lighten his vocal production to imitate the vocal timbre he desires. To wit, vocal imitations given by professional mimics can produce, with their single set of vocal muscles, a wide variety of sounds. Undoubtedly, their vocal mechanisms are capable of great flexibility in thickening and thinning the approximation of the cords to reproduce this wide range of sounds. Many young singers tend to imitate the sounds of singers whom they particularly admire, especially if the voice they wish to reproduce has been influential to them: parents, vocal instructors or famous singers. Therefore, voice classification only by timbre may be

174

an erroneous means of identifying the true category of the voice.

However, there is a more certain means of voice classification. After the teacher has helped the student to achieve a relatively secure focus of his or her voice, it is very necessary to note where the passaggio lies. The actual change in vocal production will vary in scope as well as in degree. Some singers possessing a great deal of muscular flexibility will be able to negotiate the notes over this area of their vocal range with significant ease, while others tend to "break" and, thus, "croak" or yodel into a falsetto. This, of course, is most evident in male voices when they approach the upper region of their range. (One reason why there are so few tenors in the world is that many so-called baritones have failed to develop the passaggio area of their voices to allow them to sing from e^1 to g^1 with any degree of security and thus, utilize their "head voices.")

The following voice classifications according to the passaggio has been of great value to me in determining voice classification. (Note that the passaggio may vary both in scope and actual area of notes depending upon the time of day, vocal condition or ascending-descending notes of a given passage.)

Bass, B (immediately below middle c on the piano) to d^1

Bass-baritone, c^1 (middle c on the piano) to d^1

Baritone, d^1 to e^1

Dramatic (Helden) tenor, e^1 to f^1

Lyric tenor, f^1 to g^1

Contralto, a^1 to b^1 or c^2

Mezzo-soprano, c^2 to d^2, and frequently e^1 to f^1

Dramatic soprano, e^1 to f^1 and slight adjustment usually at e^2 and f^2

Lyric coloratura soprano, e^1 to f^1

Coloratura soprano, f^1 to g^1

Note that the tenor passaggio occurs over precisely the same notes as the soprano. The difference is that the tenor passaggio occurs in the upper region of the vocal range, whereas the soprano change occurs at the bottom of her normal singing range. Thus, one can easily deduce that the soprano sings mostly in her "head voice" whereas the other categories (particularly men) sing more frequently in the "chest voice" range. It is important to emphasize again that the tenor tessitura frequently lies over the passaggio, i.e., e^1 to g^1 in vocal literature. This is one of the major reasons why tenors have so many vocal problems. We should recognize that the so-called "chest voice" in women, particularly sopranos, is usually weak and ineffective, when the musculature is undeveloped, whereas the tenor's "head voice" or falsetto is also weak and ineffective when undeveloped to its full potential. Thus, it behooves sopranos and tenors to concentrate on strengthening these respective areas of their voices to be able to extend their ranges. (By soprano "chest voice" I do not mean a raspy sound; rather a fuller, more fundamental sound when singing below f^1. Therefore, it is significant to note that all too many sopranos carry the "head voice" down below their vocal change and experience significant weakness of tone from e^1 or f^1 down to lower pitches. Throughout this transition area sopranos must engage some degree of the "chest voice" (gradually more and more) as they descend below these notes. (Mozart, who wrote many of his arias for the male soprano voice, utilized a very wide range--usually from A below c^1 to f^3.) "Chest voice" production in the soprano singer always must be coupled with a slight "lift" of the soft palate in order to add warmth to the tone and avoid causing harm to the vocal mechanism.

I dislike the use of the term "cover" to indicate that darkening or changing the singer's concept of the vowel (migrating from the clear "core" of the vowel sound) can achieve a smooth transition over the passaggio. This approach to solving problems of the transition into the head voice causes tension in the vocal musculature and, quite naturally, adversely affects diction. Dr. Brodnitz states: "Covering has to be used with great care, because, in its extreme form, it is hard on voices."[2]

To be certain, the net effect of the vowels produced over the passaggio (as well as in the "head voice") of the alto, tenor or bass voice may be darker than the vowels produced in the lower and medium range of those voices. That is simply effect--not cause. If a singer thinks of producing dark-sounding vowels (as the term "cover" implies), he will surely produce "woofy," muddy tones. In contrast, the singer should begin to gradually "elminate the mass" of the vocal folds as he ascends to his upper range (i.e., imagining the lighter texture of the falsetto or "head voice" in those tones which embrace that part of the vocal range). In conjunction with this effort, he must make a special attempt to produce a clear, forward-focused vowel. The result will be a "cleaner" tone with good diction as an added bonus. I encourage my students to "think in stereo" over the passaggio area of the vocal range, i.e., having an aural image of both timbres of vocal quality simultaneously.

Thus, singers should be warned not to confuse cause and effect. To be certain, the vowel sounds on tones in the upper vocal range sound more alike than those in the lower range. However, the focal point of the pure vowel sound always should be clearly defined in the singer's mind, and by adding space (enough yawn), the effect will be a mellowing of the tone that can be termed "cover" to the listener.

References

[1] Weldon Whitlock, Profiles in Vocal Pedagogy (Ann Arbor, Mich.: Clifton Press, 1975), p. 25.

[2] Friedrich Brodnitz, Keep Your Voice Healthy (New York: Harper Bros., 1953), p. 83.

APPENDIX

The following examples are specific applications of the Vowel Spectrum to songs. Note the simplicity of application to the languages illustrated, the purpose being to adapt the most instinctive, uncomplicated symbols to the process of singing. Only the basic vowel sounds are indicated; other vanishing sounds of diphthongs are not indicated, because they are quite naturally employed by the singer in his normal speech patterns.

It may be helpful to the reader to refer to the Vowel Spectrum (page 69) in applying these basic symbols to the following songs as well as other literature to be studied.

Nachwirkung.

Alfred Meissner.

Mit Genehmigung des Original-Verleger Barth. Senff. Leipzig.   A. J. B. 1792

A. J. B. 1792

181

GIULIO CACCINI

101915-18

APPENDIX

Nº 18. – AIR FOR SOPRANO
"REJOICE GREATLY, O DAUGHTER OF ZION!"

Zechariah ix: 9,10

APPENDIX

APPENDIX

187

GLOSSARY

ABDOMINAL BREATHING   The expansion of the abdominal and lower back muscles upon inhalation. These muscles also essentially control the exhalation of breath during the singing process.

ABDUCTION   The processes of drawing the vocal folds apart by the rear cricoarytenoid muscles (see page 39).

ADDUCTION   The process of drawing the vocal folds together by the lateral and interarytenoid muscles (see page 40).

AMPLIFIER   All of the cavities of the throat and head, which amplify the sounds produced by the vocal bands.

ANTRUM   Sinus cavities in the upper jaw which open into the nasal passages.

ARYTENOID CARTILAGES   Two small laryngeal cartilages, which open and close the vocal folds. (See pages 25ff and 39 for illustration of their action.)

AURAL IMAGE   The mental concept of the tone before it is produced by the singer; the imagining of the sound as it "feels," rather than as one hears it through the Eustachian tubes. Ideally, the aural image of the tone should become a subconscious process.

BEL CANTO   A much abused term among vocalists and voice teachers, literally meaning "beautiful singing."

BLEAT   A very rapid vibrato.

BRASSY TONES   Those vocal pitches which emphasize the higher partials of the tones over the lower partials.

BREAK   The note(s) on which the vocal folds must make a major adjustment from one "register" of the voice to

191

GLOSSARY

another. Ideally, the voice should not "break" at any
point in the singer's range (see especially pp. 33-38).

BREATH COLUMN   The column of air which passes through
the vocal folds to produce sound; also conceived of as
the means by which sound vibrations are transmitted
through space.

BRONCHIAL TUBES   "Hoses" which transmit air to the
lungs.

BUCCALPHARYNGEAL CAVITY   The area which includes
the entire mouth, soft palate, hard palate and the lips.

CAVITY   A chamber which amplifies sound.

CHEST VOICE   Commonly termed the lower range of any
voice--as opposed to "head" voice, the upper range of
any voice; named "chest" because the physical sensation
of resonance feels as if it emanates from the chest.
(See HEAD VOICE.)

CLAVICULAR BREATHING   The raising of the shoulders
when inhaling; the ascending of the entire clavicular
area.

CONSONANT   A speech sound characterized in enunciation
by constriction of the breath channel as distinguished
from the vowel, which is identified by the resonance
form of the vocal cavities.

COVER   A term having at least three meanings: (1) to
"darken" the tone (make the sound less white or bright)
by focusing the tone in the posterior of the buccalpharyngeal cavity, (2) the adjustment of the vowel toward a
duller sound, which in turn, is claimed to provide a
vehicle for transition over the passaggio, (3) forming
a closed vowel.

CRICOARYTENOID MUSCLES   Those vocal muscles which
must be employed in singing in the upper range of the
voice. (See pages 40-41.)

CRICOID CARTILAGE   The base on which the larynx rests.

DEEPLY-SET VOWEL   The formation of the buccalpharyngeal

192

cavity in a narrow vowel formation (not spread and
wide), but also not focused back in the throat.

DIAPHRAGM   A membrane shaped like an inverted bowl,
which draws air into the lungs. (See pages 55-56.)

DIAPHRAGMATIC BREATHING   Use of the external muscles
in the area of the diaphragm, avoiding significant action
of the clavicle and abdominal areas.

DIPHTHONG   A complex speech sound beginning with one
speech sound and moving (migrating) to another vowel
or semivowel position within the same syllable [Ameri-
can Heritage Dictionary, 1969].

EPIGLOTTIS   A thin plate of yellow elastic cartilage attached to the base of the tongue which folds back over
and covers the windpipe allowing food to pass through
the esophagus to the stomach rather than into the lungs
when swallowing.

EUSTACHIAN TUBE   A bony and cartilaginous tube which is
connected to the nasopharynx. It transmits sound from
the mouth to the ear and is more readily termed the
"auditory tube."

FALSETTO   Literally, a false tone in the upper "register"
of the male voice, and produced by a very light approximation of the vocal folds. (See pages 117-121.) El-
son's Music Dictionary defines it as the male head
voice as distinguished from the chest voice.

FORWARD   Referring to a sensation of sound or vowel as
being principally focused on the hard palate and/or
upper front teeth; those sounds which produce the higher
partials (see OVERTONES).

GLISSANDO   Continued tone production while singing from
one note to another some distance away (usually an
octave or more).

GLOTTAL STROKE   Sudden "explosion" of tone, by tensing
the vocalis muscles to the point at which the breath
forces the folds to part suddenly.

GLOSSARY

GRAND SCALE CC (2 octaves below middle c on the piano), C, c^1, c^2, c^3, etc.

HEAD VOICE Commonly termed the upper range of any voice--as opposed to "chest" voice, the lower range of any voice; named "head" because the physical sensation of resonance feels as if it emanates from the head. (See CHEST VOICE.)

MELISMA A series of notes sung on one syllable.

MODIFIED VOWELS Vowel sounds that are slightly altered in pronunciation from the main set, such as the open Italian "oh," or the "Ah" sound in "mother." (See Vowel Spectrum, page 69.)

MUDDLED VOWEL A vowel that lacks focus in sound and definition (also referred to as "muddy").

NARROW VOWEL SHAPE A deeply-set vowel which avoids spreading. (See pages 75-76.)

NASOPHARYNX The pharyngeal area behind the nose.

OPEN THROAT The oral pharynx expanded so as to approximate what one feels at the beginning of a yawn.

ORAL PHARYNX The rear mouth area which includes the soft palate.

OVERTONES Sound vibrations (frequencies) heard above the fundamental tone, also called "partials."

PALATE, HARD The bony structure of the mouth in which the teeth are imbedded.

PALATE, SOFT The rear, soft tissue of the mouth, which has muscles to change its shape and size, thus accommodating vowel and tonal colors.

PASSAGGIO The "passageway" between the lower and upper vocal ranges.

PEDAGOGY Systematized learning or instruction concerning principles and methods of teaching [Webster's Collegiate Dictionary, 1961].

194

GLOSSARY

PHARYNX   The section of the digestive tract that extends from the nasal cavities to the larynx, thus becoming continuous with the esophagus. The pharynx envelops three areas--the laryngo-pharynx, oral pharynx and naso-pharynx. (See page 25, fig. 1.)

PHONATION   The process of activating the vocal folds into sound-production.

PHONETIC   Representing sounds of speech with a set of distinct symbols, such denoting a single sound [American Heritage Dictionary, 1969].

PRINCIPAL VOWELS   EE, AY, AH, OH, OO. (See Vowel Spectrum, page 69.)

REGISTERS   In crude states of vocal production the sound, which produces distinctly different timbres, can be termed "register. " Some pedagogs refer to three: "chest, " "middle" (or "mixed") and "head" (or "falsetto").

RELEASE   A term used to connote the absence of tension, rather than "relax," which tends to imply limpness. In singing there must be a sense of firmness, but not muscular rigidity.

RESONANCE   The intensification and prolongation of sound, especially of a musical tone, produced by sympathetic vibration [American Heritage Dictionary, 1969].

SCHWA [ə]   An intermediate sound in many unstressed syllables; a short or indistinct sound [American Heritage Dictionary, 1969].

SHALLOW VOWEL   A vowel produced by a buccalpharyngeal formation which is inadequate in size and shape to properly amplify the sound produced by the vocal folds.

SNARL   A term used to illustrate for the vocalist that he should raise the upper lip slightly in order to bring the tonal focus forward in the mask; used nearly synonymously with the term "sneer. " The concept is used to avoid the wide "smile," which often causes tones to spread and lack focus or "point. "

195

GLOSSARY

SPINAL CURVATURE   Equivalent to "sway-back."

STEREO EFFECT   A term used to indicate to the singer that he must "hear" or "feel" the sounds of the lower and upper ranges of his voice simultaneously as he crosses his passaggio.

SUB-VOWELS   Liquid consonants, such as m, n, (ng), l, r (uhr), v and z, termed by this writer as being "sub-vowel" sounds in singing, because they may actually be identified with a given pitch to at least some degree.

THORAX   The part of the anatomy between the neck and diaphragm, partially encased by the ribs; the chest [American Heritage Dictionary, 1969].

THROAT   Often confused with the back of the mouth, but referred to in this book as the area between the uvula and the larynx; termed the "oral pharynx."

THROATY SOUND   A dark or muffled sound devoid of any bright quality; appearing to be focused only in the oral pharynx.

TONAL FOCUS   The sensation of achieving a "point" of the tone produced in which the amplification of vocal sound seems to achieve its optimum resonance.

TRACHEA   Wind pipe.

TREMOLO   A very wide vibrato in which the actual pitch seems to be uncertain.

TRIPHTHONG   Three identifiable sounds found in some English words of nominally one syllable; an example is "pure"--PEE-OO-UHR.

UVULA   The appendage of the soft palate, which protrudes downward.

VANISHING SOUNDS   The second sound of a diphthong which tends to vanish in ordinary speech patterns ("gay," AY-ee; "go," OH-oo).

VELUM   The soft palate (literally "veil").

196

GLOSSARY

VENTRICLE OF MORGANI   The chamber in the larynx just above the vocal folds, identified in Gray's Anatomy as the laryngeal sinus, and named after its discoverer. (See Fig. 12, page 41.)

VIBRATOR   The vocal folds.

VOCAL MASS   The thickness of the vocal folds as they are approximated in phonation.

VOCAL MECHANISM   The vocal folds, muscles, cartilages and bones, which function in the throat and mouth area in the production of vocal sounds.

VOWEL   A speech sound created by a relatively free passage of breath through the larynx and oral cavity, usually forming the most prominent and central sound of a syllable [American Heritage Dictionary, 1969].

VOWEL DERIVATIVE   A vowel sound in English drawn from the principal vowels--ih, eh, aah, aw, uuh and uhr. (See Vowel Spectrum, page 69.)

VOWEL DIFFUSION   A weak tone derived from a "flabby" oral pharynx.

VOWELING   A term used to denote vowel production.

VOWEL SPECTRUM   A chart outlining the vowel sounds in easily applied form as in contrast to the International Phonetic Alphabet; the range of audible vowel sounds which give definition to a language. (See page 69.)

YAWNING SENSATION   In singing, the position of the oral pharynx experienced as one begins to yawn.

ZIPPER ACTION   A concept which describes a general action of the vocal folds as they ascend and descend the scale of pitches.

197

INDEX

199

INDEX